LIVES OF MODERN WOMEN

General Editor: Emma Tennant

Jean Rhys

Carole Angier

VIKING

VIKING

Penguin Books Ltd, Harmondsworth, Middlesex, England
Viking Penguin Inc., 40 West 23rd Street, New York, New York 10010, U.S.A.
Penguin Books Australia Ltd, Ringwood, Victoria, Australia
Penguin Books Canada Ltd, 2801 John Street, Markham, Ontario, Canada L3R 1B4
Penguin Books (N.Z.) Ltd, 182–190 Wairau Road, Auckland 10, New Zealand

First published 1985
Published simultaneously in Penguin Books

Made and printed in Great Britain by
Richard Clay (The Chaucer Press) Ltd,
Bungay, Suffolk
Set in Monophoto Photina

British Library Cataloguing in Publication Data

Angier, Carole
 Jean Rhys.—(Lives of modern women)
 1. Rhys, Jean—Biography   2. Novelists,
 English—20th century—Biography
 I. Title   II. Series
 813   PR6035.H96Z/

ISBN 0–670–80626–9

Library of Congress Catalog Card Number: 85–51189

CONTENTS

CONTENTS

NOTES AND ACKNOWLEDGEMENTS

All the thoughts and feelings attributed to Jean Rhys in this book are quoted from or based on things she said or wrote, or things that have been said or written about her. As well as her published novels, stories, autobiography and letters, I have used her notes and drafts for these; I have also drawn upon unpublished manuscripts, notes and drafts in the British Museum and in the possession of her literary executor, Francis Wyndham.

I would like to express my special debt and thanks to Francis Wyndham, for his unfailing help and generosity; to Diana Athill of André Deutsch, for sharing her insight into Jean and her work; to Mrs Phyllis Smyser, for sharing her memories of her father, Leslie Tilden Smith; to Oliver Stoner, for his excellent criticism; and to Diana Melly, for all her help. Finally, I would like to express special thanks to Jean's daughter, Mme Maryvonne Moerman-Lenglet, who has continued to be most generous with information and assistance even though she dissents at several points from my portrait of her mother.

I would also like to thank the following people for so kindly giving their time and assistance: Mr Aubrey Baring; Mr Oliver Baring; Eliot Bliss; Miss Janet Bridger; my typist, Mrs Helen Burnett; Mrs Joan Butler; Miss Heather Cubitt (Head of History, Perse School); Lady Antonia Fraser; Michael Henshaw; George Melly; Miss Gwen Neal (Old Girls' Association, Perse School); Mr Richard O'Donoghue (Administrator–Registrar, Royal Academy of Dramatic Art); Diana Petre; David Plante; Group Capt. L. E. Robins; Mr Julian Martin Smith; Mrs Oliver Stoner.

24 August 1890	Birth of Ella Gwendolen Rees Williams at Roseau, Dominica. She had two older brothers, Edward and Owen; an older sister, Minna; and a younger sister, Brenda.
1907–8	The Perse School, Cambridge.
1909	The Academy of Dramatic Art.
1909–10	Two and a half tours in the chorus of *Our Miss Gibbs*.
1910–12	Her first affair.
1913	Her 'illegal operation'. For the next six years she lives mainly on her first lover's allowance.
1914	In January she writes her first diary.
1914–17	Voluntary work at a soldiers' canteen.
1917	Meets Jean Lenglet.
1918	Works in pensions office.

1919	Marries Jean Lenglet and goes to Paris. 29 December, birth of their son, William Owen. Three weeks later he dies of pneumonia.
1920–22	Vienna and Budapest.
1922	Birth of their daughter, Maryvonne. Jean meets Ford Madox Ford and begins to write short stories.
1923–4	Jean Lenglet in prison. Affair with Ford. In December 1924 Ford publishes *Vienne* in the *transatlantic review*.
1925–6	Jean writes *Quartet*.
1927	*The Left Bank* published. Jean returns to England, meets Leslie Tilden Smith.
1928	*Quartet* published (as *Postures*).
1930s	Jean publishes *After Leaving Mr Mackenzie* (1930), *Voyage in the Dark* (1934), *Good Morning, Midnight* (1939). She also writes short stories, autobiographical reminiscences, and the first version of *Wide Sargasso Sea*, called *Le Revenant*.
1932	Divorce from Jean Lenglet.
1934	Marriage to Leslie Tilden Smith.
1936	Visit to Dominica.
1940s	Norfolk and London. Jean writes short stories.
2 October 1945	Death of Leslie Tilden Smith.

1947	Marriage to Max Hamer.
1949	In May Jean is convicted of assault; she spends five days in the hospital wing of Holloway Prison. In November Selma Vaz Dias traces Jean for the first time.
1950	Max arrested for cheque fraud.
1950–52	Max in Maidstone Prison; Jean lives in Maidstone.
1952–6	London.
1956–60	Cornwall. In October 1960 the last move, to Cheriton Fitzpaine in Devon.
1957	Selma traces Jean again; performs *Good Morning, Midnight* on BBC radio. Francis Wyndham writes to Jean, and André Deutsch buy the option on *Wide Sargasso Sea*.
1957–66	Jean works on *Wide Sargasso Sea*. Max's health deteriorates; Jean herself has a heart attack in 1964.
7 March 1966	Death of Max Hamer. Jean finally releases *Wide Sargasso Sea* to the publisher.
1966	*Wide Sargasso Sea* published.
1967	*Wide Sargasso Sea* wins W. H. Smith & Son Annual Literary Award.
1967–73	All Jean's novels reissued by André Deutsch and published in paperback by Penguin.

CHRONOLOGY

1968	*Tigers are Better Looking.*
1976	*Sleep It Off Lady.*
1978	Jean receives CBE.
March 1979	Jean's last fall.
14 May 1979	Death of Jean Rhys.
1979	*Smile Please.*
1984	*Jean Rhys: Letters 1931–66*, edited by Francis Wyndham and Diana Melly.

INTRODUCTION

Jean Rhys was not a modern woman. Modern women want their own independent lives and independent souls – and these were the last things Jean wanted. From beginning to end, dependence was her way of life. It didn't bring her the peace and happiness she imagined; on the contrary, it failed her and tormented her – and she wrote about its torments. But she never gave up her ideal of it. She never wanted to be a writer, she said: all she wanted to be was an ordinary, happy, passive and protected woman.

It is, of course, her writing that is modern. Her heroines are modern: homeless and alone, in a shifting, uncertain, dangerous world. And her voice is utterly modern: moody and disillusioned, honest and mocking. Three of her five novels are set between the wars, and they have the glamour and self-destructiveness of the twenties, the poverty and anxiety of the thirties. Nonetheless, the source of Jean's deepest and most lasting attitudes is to be found farther back: Edwardian England, into which she stepped, at seventeen, alone and unprepared. Here were the arrogance and snobbery she would hate all her life. Here were the extremes of beauty and squalor, wealth and destitution, which always fascinated and frightened her. And here were the ideals of courage and loyalty, the old-world courtesy, the love of luxury, which became hers for the rest of her life. Her lucid, disabused tone, her dispossession and alienation, were modern: but her ideas and aspirations were old-fashioned. Jean's ideal was not the flapper, with her boyish haircut, her short skirts, her desire to shock; nor was it the working girl, with her trousers and her equality. It was much more the Gaiety Girl: her fragile, childlike beauty, her lovely long dresses and piled-up, scented hair, her supper by gaslight in a private restaurant room. This strange, piquant mixture of weary experience and childlike romance, of tough talk and soft hopes, is inimitable Jean Rhys.

And so she balanced on the edge of the twentieth century, and had a love–hate affair with change. She loved a picture-book England of woods and fields, snow and fires, stability and ease. She hated the complacency and cruelty it bred, but she hated squalor and meanness even more. She didn't really want the old world swept away: she just wanted it to take into its security people like her. When it wouldn't, she did long for the new world: but as soon as she saw it, she was afraid it was worse than the old.

Even as a writer, then, Jean Rhys is only partly modern. Rather, she is timeless. For she explored her own age, its moods and changes, almost by accident. What she set out to explore were her own very personal feelings. We see the outside world through them, but only reflected and distorted by her concentration on what really concerned her: her own life, and her own suffering. She was entirely self-absorbed. She cut everything out of her writing but herself; and in order to write she did the same to her life. She became a near-recluse; though she suffered intensely from their separation, she never lived an ordinary family life with her daughter. As she grew older she pared more and more away in her writing – her present husbands, her present surroundings – so that all that was left were her deepest experience and her deepest feelings, and they were always the same. These experiences are what she wrote about over and over again, seeing herself and them more clearly each time: experiences of love and rejection, hate and revenge, fatality and fear.

Necessarily, therefore, Jean Rhys's novels are autobiographical: Not autobiographical in every detail, as readers sometimes suppose, but autobiographical they were, says Diana Athill, Jean's editor and friend. They had to be, because her whole aim was to find out the truth about her life. 'Such terrible things happen,' says Antoinette, her last heroine. 'Why? Why?' It was to answer that question that Jean wrote all her books: to understand, and to exorcize, her suffering. And to do that she had to stay very close to her experience. She cut, shaped and ordered it; she changed details and unimportant facts. But she stayed true to the essence of each experience. 'I can't make things up, I can't invent,' she said. 'I just write about what happened. Not that my books are entirely my life – but almost.' They were the most important parts of her life: each heroine is herself at one important stage of her experience. We not only can identify Jean with her heroines: we must do.

Following the heroines through the novels and stories, therefore, is following Jean's journey into self-knowledge – which is the point of all her life and work. She didn't publish the story of the youngest heroine, Anna, first, but she did write it first, in a diary on which she based *Voyage in the Dark*. Once Jean has got herself to England, therefore, we too will start with Anna; we will follow her through Marya and Julia, to see why she ended up as Sasha, the oldest heroine. It took Jean all her writing life to explore the reasons; it wasn't until she went back to childhood, with Antoinette, that she could tell the whole story.

But of course even Antoinette leaves out one part of Jean's story, and that the most important: the story of the writer. That one she never wrote. The self she wanted to understand was not the writer but the woman – the woman who longed to be happy, and who was so unhappy. This gap between Jean and her heroines grew as she grew older, as she wrote more and more, and as the experiences she wrote about receded into the past. They were essentially the experiences of her first three and a half decades: from about 1927, therefore, when she returned to England and began to publish, we shall look at her life more and more separately from the lives of her heroines.

When one of those heroines, Julia, goes to see her ex-lover, Neil

James, he doesn't want to hear what has happened to her. 'My dear,' he says, 'don't harrow me.' Jean's story *is* harrowing. She had been given a supreme gift of knowing how to write; she had not been given the gift of knowing how to live. She railed unceasingly against this fate. She didn't want admiration as a writer; she wanted love and acceptance and belonging as a woman. She never found them – or if she did they were shadowed by fear, and soon over. Her nature was full of contradictions and weaknesses; she was racked all her life by terrible demons. Against all of them she never stopped fighting, with extraordinary resilience and courage, for nearly ninety years. She fought with wit and self-mockery; she fought with moments of pleasure and friendship; she fought above all by writing. Her life was unbearably sad: only her art was triumphant.

CHAPTER ONE

Overture and Beginners Please: 1907–9

i. *Overture*

In August 1907 Jean Rhys arrived at Southampton from Dominica. Her name was Gwen Williams then, and she was a week or two short of seventeen.

It was a grey day, but she was filled with enormous excitement and hopefulness. At home she had felt that she didn't belong, that what she wanted wasn't there; and then she would think, 'Perhaps in England I'll find it.' From books and pictures and songs she had built up an idea of England in her mind. It would be strange and wonderful, full of snow and hail – what *was* hail? – and city streets; the streets would be full of beautiful, elegant women, on the arms of tall men with quiet voices and an easy, assured way of walking. Now she was here. Her English aunt took her to Westminster Abbey, St Paul's, the Zoo. 'Don't you think it's wonderful?' she said. But for Gwen Williams it had all gone wrong. The first, the worst disappointment had happened: England had let her down.

'Nothing was as grand as I thought it would be': instead,

everything was small and mean. The people on the streets were not rich and elegant, but poor and ugly. She had heard wonderful stories of the London theatre from her Auntie B. But when she went to a play she saw the backcloth move: it was only painted.

She thought all the time, 'Of course, this isn't England. I'm going to see England suddenly. Of course this isn't it.' For brief moments she saw it – in the snow, in the marvellous shops, in a few lovely girls. She would be like them. She would be an actress, like the ones she saw on posters – 'and perhaps a *fille de joie*' too, because the words were so beautiful.

But now England baffled and bewildered her. On her first morning in London she slipped out of her Bloomsbury boarding house for a walk. When she came back, she lay in a hot bath and began to feel happy. And again things went wrong. The landlady was angry, her aunt was very angry. 'You are quite incapable of thinking about anyone else but yourself,' she said. Did Gwen not realize that she had taken all the hot water? – but she didn't. Indoor lavatories were a shock to her, plumbing a mystery. She didn't know, she didn't understand, and no one told her. That was what she felt about England.

Now she had to go to school, and that too started as badly as possible. Aunt Clarice took her to Swan and Edgar's to buy clothes. She fell in love with a beautiful wine-coloured suit, with a three-quarter length coat and a grey fur collar. But Aunt Clarice said, 'The things you want are far too expensive,' and bought her a dark blue one instead, very hairy, with brass buttons. She thought about appearing before a lot of strange girls in that hideous garment, and felt very miserable. 'They're bound to dislike me,' she thought.

She arrived at the Perse High School for Girls in the autumn of 1907. She was shy and hopeless. She couldn't play hockey or ride a bicycle; she felt clumsy and ignorant. At first she asked questions and tried to learn. But the girls laughed and said, 'Poor West Indies, you'll believe anything'; so she soon stopped asking. Then they pretended to ask her questions.

'Is it "honey don't try so hard" or "honey don't cry so hard"?'

'How should I know?'

'Well, it's a coon song, you ought to know.'

Winks, smiles. That's what she remembered.

When they asked, 'Why did they send you to the old Perse if they were so fond of you?' she answered, 'Because my English aunt said it was a good school.' But a good school in Edwardian England was not a happy place for her. In 1907 the Perse was strict and spartan: no carpets, no flowers, no pictures, just wooden desks and benches, and narrow beds for the boarders. The mistresses were formidable Cambridge women, very different from the gentle nuns of Roseau. Gwen Williams's flashing, instinctive, romantic mind did not appeal to them. Even when she won the school prize in Roman History, they knew (she thought) that it was only because she had read *Quo Vadis*.

But when she was angry she fought back. In her second term there was a debate on the resolution that 'The popularity of modern literature, to the exclusion of standard works, is unreasonable and deplorable'. This sort of piety

21

made her laugh, and she was already like Julia in *After Leaving Mr Mackenzie*: 'Because she felt such contempt her nervousness left her.' 'She expressed her views fearlessly,' said the *Persean Magazine*. It was her first public attempt to defend her point of view. Later she forgot all about it – she never wrote of it, or mentioned it to anyone. But in her novels she went on defending herself in the same way, and with the same result. It was only 1908, but already the respectable world's verdict on her life and works lay waiting, curled up like a snake in the pen of the schoolgirl reporter. The Hon. Member, she said, 'needs to take a less flippant view of things in general ... Daring and originality are always welcomed in a speech, but they must not be confounded with exaggeration.'

Gwen Williams's side was only narrowly defeated, but that too she forgot. Only when she felt outnumbered and defeated could she break free of her timidity and find the energy to act, to write, to live. And so she felt outnumbered and defeated. What made her feel most defeated was disapproval – disapproval, therefore, was what she remembered. She remembered the headmistress, Miss Street, and her friend, Miss Osborn, who had founded the school together a quarter of a century before. In her story 'Overture and Beginners Please' she remembers that 'Miss Rode' was kind to her: but she remembers 'Miss Born' much more. Miss Born hated her. Miss Born made her read aloud, and then said her voice was too high; Miss Born said to Miss Rode, 'Why did you insist on that girl playing Autolycus? Tony Lumpkin in person.' She had played Autolycus in her first term, and was proud of her success – Miss Born's remark was a mean, uncalled-for sneer . . . She forgot that she had also played Tony Lumpkin, the next year, to even greater success. ('Gwen Williams, as Tony, carried off the palm,' said the the *Persean*. 'Tony was a triumph.') No doubt 'Miss Born' did disapprove of her – people in authority usually did. But whatever that remark was, it wasn't simply an insult. It was just that she forgot everything about it except the insult. It hurt more then: but then too Miss Osborn, who was a real person she could never understand, became Miss Born, who she knew was a monster – and she could fight back.

Gwen was at school for four terms, and had only two happy memories. One was of Ely Cathedral, which made her tremble with excitement. The other was of being knocked down by an undergraduate on a bicycle. This was 'by far my nicest Cambridge memory': 'I wasn't hurt but he picked me up so carefully and apologized so profusely that I thought about him for a long time.' At Ely she had felt mystery and grandeur; face down on the Trumpington Road she had felt the touch of a kind hand. These were the things she always wanted, and never gave up looking for.

But they weren't here. The Cambridge sky was grey-yellow, the colour of no hope, the colour of despair. She thought, 'This is all wrong for me'; she felt, 'I will always be lonely, I will never get away'; she asked herself, 'Why am I here at all?' The answer came to her in a letter from a girl who had already left school, and whom she hardly remembered. 'This letter changed my life and I can still remember most of it,' she wrote, when she was over eighty. The girl's name was Myrtle Newton. 'Dear West Indies,' Myrtle wrote, 'I see now what a lot of silly fools we were

about everything that matters and I don't think you are.'
Myrtle's mother thought she was a born actress. 'She says
that you ought to go on the stage, and why don't you?' Yes
– that was it! She didn't reply to Myrtle's letter. Instead she
wrote straight to her father and told him she wanted to go
to the Academy of Dramatic Art.

Her father said she could go, and she was happier than
she had ever been in her life. For a time she stayed on at
school, taking extra elocution and singing lessons from a
young clergyman. He asked her why she wanted to go on
the stage.

'I love the sound of words.'

'And?'

'I like it when the audience claps, and I adore everything
to do with the stage.'

At the end of 1908 she passed her Oxford and Cambridge
Higher Certificate and went to take her entrance ex-
amination for the Academy. People said she wouldn't pass,
and though she insisted that she would she was very
nervous. She recited 'The Bells'; the judges seemed very
bored. But her luck held and she passed. She left school
without a backward look. 'Nothing could touch me, not
praise nor blame.' Aunt Clarice put her into another
Bloomsbury boarding house and left her to it.

She entered the Academy of Dramatic Art with thirty-
four other students in January 1909. Again she had set out
with high hopes; again what she remembered was dis-
comfiture and disappointment. It was like school, but worse.
This time she arrived in a skirt which was too long, so that
she had to wear it tucked up at the waist. Aunt Clarice said

she was so thin that no one would notice, but of course they all noticed straight away. Again most of the teachers ignored or disapproved of her. Her friends were foreigners like herself – an Australian girl, a half-Turkish girl – and they didn't last long. The only girl who was nice to her left, after a terrible row over the proper pronunciation of a word.

'Froth,' said the elocution master. 'Frawth,' said the pupil. For a long time they shouted at each other: 'Froth' – 'Frawth' – 'Froth' – 'Frawth'. I listened to this appalled . . . At last Honor said: 'I refuse to pronounce the word "froth". "Froth" is Cockney and I'm not here to learn Cockney.'

Honor was taken away and the elocution master left or was dismissed. 'I learnt nothing at the school of acting except the exact meaning of the word snob,' Jean wrote when she was old. She had played Celia in *As You Like It*, and Francesca in *Paolo and Francesca*, saying, 'All ties that held me I cast off.' But no ties held her. She left the Academy as she had left school, 'without a qualm'.

ii. *Beginners Please*

She spent the holiday with relatives in Yorkshire. Early one morning her uncle woke her: her father had died suddenly. At first she didn't believe him; when she did, she cried without ceasing. She was sent back to Aunt Clarice in Wales. Her aunt said, 'You cry without reticence.' 'And you watch me without reticence,' she thought.

Her mother wrote to say that she could not return to the

Academy now, and she should come home at once. But she was sure they didn't really want her back; and she didn't want to go, not yet. 'You'll have to,' said Aunt Clarice. But she wouldn't. They went to London to buy her tropical clothes, and while her aunt was visiting friends she went to Blackmore's agency and got a job in the chorus of a musical comedy. Her aunt was enraged – she had behaved deceitfully, outrageously, she said. Gwen was hurt and astonished. She couldn't understand it. She had spurned dependence and found herself a job – and look what happened. She threatened to marry a boy who had proposed to her at the Academy, and whom Aunt Clarice detested (though she hesitated when she heard he had a lot of money). 'If you interfere with my contract I'll marry him and be miserable. And it'll be your fault,' Gwen said. Aunt Clarice threw up her hands and wrote to Gwen's mother. When the answer came it was vague. Mrs Rees Williams was grieving, and worried about money; she sounded relieved that her daughter could earn her own living in England. Gwen had won.

She went to rehearse *Our Miss Gibbs* at the National Sporting Club near Leicester Square. Boxers passed through shyly, on their way to other rooms. Some of the girls were dreading the tour up north in the winter, but she hardly listened. She was excited and happy again. Perhaps at last she had found the thing that was romantic and grand; perhaps at last real life would begin.

CHAPTER TWO

Voyage in the Dark: 1909–27

i. *The Chorus*

Was it real life that started now, or was it a dream? All she knew was that it was very different.

It was as if a curtain had fallen, hiding everything I had ever known. It was almost like being born again.

Sometimes it was as if England was a dream; sometimes it was as if England was real, and her memories of childhood were the dream. But she could never fit the two together.

She was nineteen now, and from now on she was alone. Some years after her father's death her mother and sisters came to England, but she rarely saw them. And she no longer shared their name. In the chorus she called herself Ella, or sometimes Emma, Gray; in stories, Petronella or Vivian Gray. She would change her name and her life like this several times, so that people would easily lose her and think her dead. This frightened her, but it protected her too. Anna in *Voyage in the Dark* says:

'I'll never tell you my real name and I'll never tell you anything real about myself. Everything that I tell you about myself is a lie.'

In just this way Ella Gray, when she became Jean Rhys, told the world that everything she said about herself was fiction.

In the winter of 1909 *Our Miss Gibbs* toured the north of England – Wigan, Blackburn, Bury, Oldham, Leeds, Halifax, Huddersfield, Southport . . . It was winter, and very cold. She couldn't get used to this cold, or to the way that all the towns looked exactly alike.

You were perpetually moving to another place, which was perpetually the same . . . a little grey street leading to the stage door of the theatre and another little grey street where your lodgings were.

The lodgings were always the same, with 'a high dark wardrobe and something dirty red in the room'; and the food was always the same too. On Sunday a tough joint of beef; on Monday the beef warmed up; on Tuesday the beef minced; on Wednesday the beef in shepherd's pie or stew; on Thursday egg and bacon; on Friday pot luck; and on Saturday nothing, as they packed and left for another town. She met girls with names like Billie and Daisie, Maudie and Laurie. *They* weren't all the same. Some aimed to get on in the theatre, or to make good marriages; others were more or less tarts. Ella Gray sometimes envied the ambitious ones, but she didn't really like them. She liked the tarts. She liked the way Laurie sounded impatient but was kind underneath: 'Can't you manage to keep the door shut, Virgin, you silly cow?' And she liked the way Maudie wasn't fooled by people who sounded kind but weren't: 'I bet she puts that down on the bill,' Maudie would say. 'For saying "Good morning", half a crown.' She liked their slang – 'He must be up the pole', and 'This place gives me the pip'. It was a secret language, like the ones at home – the servants' patois, or the Carib women's language, which the men didn't know. She was secretly shocked by their coarse jokes, for on the other side of the curtain that had now fallen she had been an innocent, protected girl. But she was impressed by their world-weariness, and more than half believed their cynicism: 'The thing with men is to get everything you can out of them and not care a damn.' 'The more you swank the better.' Their stoicism and fatalism, their satirical eye, their professional femininity and love of a good time, all became part of her own point of view. Their humour and their recklessness especially had a defiance that she recognized as her own – passive and pliant, but only until there was nothing left to lose. 'There's only one thing to do about this,' says Billie, when their landlady hands them an enormous bill. 'Here's to it' – and she jumps out of the window. Ella Gray is frightened, but she jumps too. Then they're running out of the gate and laughing, and Billie tosses back over her shoulder, 'One word to you!' This is the chorus girl note: it entered Ella Gray's voice, and stayed in Jean Rhys's.

But the real life of a chorus girl, earning 'thirty-five bob a week and of course extra for extra matinées', was too hard for her. In 1909 and 1910 she did two and half tours: a winter tour, a summer tour, and half a winter one again. On her first winter tour she got pleurisy, like Anna in *Voyage in the Dark*. Between tours there was always a scramble for money, and sometimes she had to live in the 'Cats' Home' – the chorus girls' hostel. In one such break she joined the chorus of a music hall sketch, '*Chanteclair*, or *Hi Cockalorum*, a Feathered Fantasy in Three Fits'. Joe Peterman, its writer and manager, had taken the title from a current Paris hit. But he had taken little else. *Chanteclair* was third-rate, the company poorly rehearsed.

Ella Gray and four or five other girls called themselves 'Liska's Troupe', and did a little dance of their own in which they pretended to lay eggs. They opened in a cold northern town. As soon as Liska's Troupe began their dance, Ella Gray felt the mockery and scorn come up from the audience like smoke. The girl beside her went on bravely laying eggs, but there was 'something as unstable as water' in Ella Gray: she simply dropped off the end of the line, and left the stage. The next day Mr Peterman demanded to know why she had walked out in the middle of her act. Was she ill? No, she was frightened. Of what? Of the audience. He said, 'And what the hell are you doing on the stage, if you are frightened of an audience?'

She went back to *Our Miss Gibbs*, but she knew he was right. She was taken out of the chorus and given a line, but she was so frightened she forgot it. Sometimes she felt excited, but never happy. Half of her was like the other girls – waiting, drifting, not even reading, except for one romantic novel called *The Forest Lovers* which they all discussed endlessly. But the other half of her remained alone: bored and lonely, a stranger looking on. She was tired of *Our Miss Gibbs*, tired of her old Gaiety dresses, worn and cleaned to shadows. And it was winter again; all the grey-stone promenades ran down to the same grey-brown or grey-green sea. She was cold – always so *cold* . . . So once again she ran away. With another girl she left the tour, and went to London. She got a job in the pantomime at the Old Lyceum Theatre. It was *Cinderella*: on stage there was an elaborate glass coach, and real ponies; in the dressing room there were rats. Going from room to room in cold dark England, she had still felt an absolute certainty that something exciting, even glorious, was waiting for her. It had not been the stage: that was a mistake. She knew now what it was.

ii. *Love*

Of course you've always known, always remembered, and then you forget so utterly, except that you've always known it.

This is what Anna thinks in *Voyage in the Dark*, when at last she lies beside her first lover. *That* was what she had wanted: warmth, his arms around her, words of love.

When Anna first met Walter she hadn't liked him; when he sniffed at the wine and sent it back she even hated him. When she pushed him away he said, 'I'm very sorry. That was extremely stupid of me,' and looked at her as though she wasn't there. But then he sent her a bunch of violets that smelt like rain, and twenty-five pounds. 'I'm worried about you,' he wrote. 'Will you buy yourself some stockings with this? And don't look anxious while you are buying them, please.' Then when she was ill he brought her an eiderdown and wine and grapes and soup, and sent his doctor to her. Her room grew bigger; and when his hand touched her face she couldn't remember that once she hadn't even liked him.

When he put money into her handbag she should have said, 'Don't do that,' but instead she said, 'Anything you like, any way you like.'

She lay in his bed and thought of the slave list she had seen once, at home: '*Maillotte Boyd, aged 18. Maillotte Boyd, aged 18 . . . But I like it like this. I don't want it any other way but this.*' It was the best way to live, because anything might happen. 'Dressing to go and meet him and coming out of the restaurant and when he kissed you in the taxi going there . . .' 'You're a perfect darling, but you're only a baby,' he said. 'Let's go upstairs, let's go upstairs. You really shock me sometimes, Miss Morgan.'

That was her life for a year and a half. Walter wanted her to get on: he paid for her to have singing lessons, he introduced her to people. But she didn't want to get on: she wanted to be with him. 'Oh, you'll soon get sick of me,' he said. 'Don't be like a stone that I try to roll up a hill and that always rolls down again.' So stupid to love someone very much, she thought. So stupid to be afraid of a thought. Well, she wouldn't think it. And she wouldn't read books, because books all say it: the man's bound to get tired.

Her lover introduced her to his cousin. He too wanted her to get on (but did that mean move on?). 'You don't mean to say you don't like Vincent?' Walter said. 'You're the only girl I've heard of who doesn't.' It was true he was handsome, more handsome than Walter, and taller and younger too. But she hated the way they looked at each other when they talked about Vincent's girl. 'It'll end in a flood of tears,'

Vincent would say. 'As usual.' Something about him made her say stupid things. 'Good night, Vincent. Thank you very much.' Then he would raise his eyebrows. 'Thank me very much? My dear child, why thank me very much?'

And in the end she didn't thank him – she had been right about him, after all. It was he who sent her the letter.

'I'm quite sure you are a nice girl and that you will be under-standing about this,' he wrote. 'Walter is still very fond of you but he doesn't love you like that any more, and after all you must always have known that the thing could not go on for ever . . . He will always be your friend and he wants to arrange that you should be provided for and not have to worry about money (for a time at any rate) . . .'

It had happened. She had known all her life that it would happen. She had been afraid for a long time, but now her fear had grown gigantic. She tried to tell Walter: 'You think I want more than I do. I only want to see you sometimes, but if I never see you again I'll die.' But she saw that he hated her for insisting on this scene, and that his caution and dis-tance had grown gigantic too. So she let go: she fell back into the water and drowned. The dream had ended, and she didn't care any more. She would never care again. She ran away from the flat without telling him where she had gone.

This affair was Ella Gray's first grab at her dream, her first gamble on getting what she wanted out of life. It was also her first and greatest loss.

Ella's real first lover was very like Walter in *Voyage in the Dark*. He was a stockbroker; he was forty to Ella's twenty; he had a house off Berkeley Square, and a handsome young cousin. But Walter was just a rather rich, rather ordinary businessman. Ella's real lover was very rich, and very upper class. When Jean Rhys wrote their story she played down her lover's wealth and position, partly in order to reduce the element of romantic dream in her novel. In real life, or in her real dream, it was very much there.

Ella's real lover was Lancelot Hugh Smith. He came from a large and distinguished family of bankers, MPs and diplomats. He was more than respectable. He did not pick up Ella as Walter had picked up Anna, on a street: he met her at a supper party. He was Eton and Cambridge; he wore wonderfully cut English clothes, and smelt of leather and smoke; he looked and sounded a completely conventional, rather philistine, entirely solid and secure member of the English establishment. He was not handsome, but to Ella he looked 'just right – always'. She loved his swinging walk, his gallant, teasing way of talking, which hid (but not from her) how much he felt. He used a secret language too, a male language of upper-class cliché – 'Kitten, your eyes are shining like stars, by Jove!' He was kind, he was elegant, he made her laugh; he bought her lovely clothes, and listened to her talk of home. He made her feel less shy. He was father, friend and lover in one – he was perfection, and she thought him a god. It seemed as if, in this first affair, she had gone straight to the heart of her dream.

She had – and yet she hadn't. Lancelot Hugh Smith looked as though he owned the world, and could make it safe for her. But underneath his beautiful clothes and upper-class manner he hid a disposition not so different from her own. He was hyper-sensitive, fastidious and nervous, and had been so all his life. He was too diffident to be successful with women. He never married: he became friend, patron, uncle, godfather, but never husband or father. He liked and admired genuinely confident young men, like his cousin Julian Martin Smith, the model for Vincent. He was – in this business of liaisons – less worldly and less decisive than Julian; he depended on him. Julian was the popular one, the charmer and the womanizer. In fact it was Julian who was the model Edwardian all the way through: handsome, brave, courteous and unimaginative; an officer and a gentleman. But Ella Gray hated him. She hated him because she thought he had urged Lancelot to leave her; but she also just hated him – for his effortless success, his easy, unquestioning belonging.

And so her dream *had* to end. Not because chorus girls couldn't marry rich respectable men – they did; but because it was a contradictory, impossible dream. She longed for someone entirely secure, yet entirely sensitive; someone utterly respectable and safe, yet able to understand her lonely, fearful, rebellious nature. Against all expectation, Lancelot really was this dream. But being so made him less, not more, able to love her and stay with her. His respectability rejected her, as she'd been afraid it would – and so did the very things that drew him to her, his own hidden loneliness and fear. Lancelot couldn't bear to see people in pain or need; he didn't even want to think about them ('My dear, don't harrow me. I don't want to hear'). As soon as he felt the real depths of Ella's need, he must have wanted to bolt.

He lived by – and achieved – the Edwardian ideals of ambition and success. ('You want to get on, don't you?'

Walter says to Anna in *Voyage in the Dark*. 'But my dear, how do you mean you don't know? Good God, you must know.') But underneath he was never sure he wanted or enjoyed them. Ella Gray knew this: 'Always the battle was going on in him between what he had been taught and what he felt.' But in *Voyage in the Dark* she smoothed it over; she made Walter merely safe, solid and philistine, because she wanted to show how the respectable world preserves itself. She was not yet ready to ask herself if the trouble lay less in him than in her dream of him. She was not yet ready to think that even English gentlemen with quiet voices and an easy way of walking might feel unsafe, and suffer.

iii. *The End of Love*

When Ella Gray's affair with Lancelot ended, she wrote a poem:

> *I didn't know*
> *I didn't know*
> *I didn't know*

She didn't know it was possible to suffer so much – to feel so black and desperate, and then so empty and unreal. For the rest of her life she felt as though some central spring of will and energy inside her had been broken: a terrible feeling of lassitude, as though she had opened her veins in a hot bath. She had only come to life when she was twenty – and by the time she was twenty-two, her life was over.

Voyage in the Dark tells what happened then. Anna met Ethel, who was a masseuse; she went to work for her as

(Ethel said) a manicurist. Ethel always talked about how respectable she was, a lady: 'A lady – some words have a long thin neck that you'd like to strangle.' On the surface everything was all right, but underneath Anna glimpsed all sorts of horrors. Then Carl came. He wasn't like her clients, nervous and hesitating: he was solid, and when he touched her she knew he was quite sure of her. So she thought, 'All right, then, I will.' She imagined him taking her away – but then she imagined him talking about her: '"I picked up a girl in London . . ." Not "girl" perhaps. Some other word, perhaps. Never mind.' After Carl left there were others. 'Going up the stairs it was pretty bad but when we got into the bedroom and had drinks it was better.' And then she was not just tired all the time but sick, and the worst of all happened.

Of course as soon as a thing has happened it isn't fantastic any more, it's inevitable. The inevitable is what you're doing or have done. The fantastic is simply what you didn't do. That goes for everybody.

Anna writes to her lover and asks for money for an abortion; instead, his cousin comes, looking fresh and clean and kind. In fact, Lancelot had found her himself; but before long he was ill, and it *was* Julian who came. Lancelot sent her a big rose plant in a pot, and a beautiful Persian kitten. But it was Julian who sent her the money, in a little canvas bag; and Julian who asked her for Lancelot's letters back, as Vincent asks for Walter's: '"Are you sure these are all?" . . . He pretended to laugh. "Well, there you are. I'm trusting you."' At the end of *Voyage in the Dark* Anna hears the doctor say, 'Ready to start all over again in no time, no doubt.' Julian's doctor said much the same thing to Ella.

The original ending of *Voyage in the Dark* suggested that Anna died aborting her child. Jean Rhys's publisher said that that was too gloomy, and with great reluctance she added the last four lines of the book, to let Anna live. But she felt that she herself had died then, with the end of her first affair – 'the real death,' as she would write in *Wide Sargasso Sea*, 'not the one people know about'. It would have been better, then, if she had died outwardly – physically – too . . . This idea sank deep into her work: that it is better to die than to go on in a living death, 'To die and be forgotten and at peace. Not to know that one is abandoned, lied about, helpless.' But she always went on.

Lancelot made her go on, now. He insisted on sending her an allowance, every week, through his solicitors. The impersonality of this felt to her worse than death. For the next six or seven years she took his money, spent it, asked for more; and all the time she hated it – and herself – and him. Once or twice she wrote to him and asked him not to send any more, because it made her so unhappy and stopped her from changing her life. But it made him even more unhappy not to send it, and in the end she always accepted it again. Besides, what could she do? She felt more and more alone, more and more useless. Her habit of reluctant, self-hating dependence had begun.

The first months of her death in life were among her worst ever, and the feelings she had then were ones she wrote about for the rest of her life. At first she found some work as a film extra; but when she had to sit for hours in a cotton dress in the dead of winter, she ran away again. After that she did nothing at all. She slept as though she were dead for as many hours as possible; the rest of the time she sat staring in front of her, or walking the grey streets like someone in a dream. She didn't care how she looked. When a man talked to her in a restaurant she saw his lips move, but didn't hear a word he said. She was frightened of how she felt – so tired, so afraid of people, thinking all the time: 'Nothing matters, nothing matters.'

Then it was Christmas. *He* sent her a Christmas tree covered in little silver and gold parcels, with a card that said 'Happy Christmas'. Looking at that tree, she knew that she would never belong anywhere; and also that she didn't *want* to belong, not to their world. She didn't want their presents or their money. She knew now what she wanted. She wanted nothing.

But suddenly someone knocked on her door – a girl she had met on her first film. Ella saw her looking at the bottle of gin on the table; she laughed loudly and admitted what she had meant to do. 'But my dear,' said the girl, 'this isn't the right house. It isn't high enough . . .' They had several gins together, and soon Ella was giggling and promising to move to Chelsea, where it wasn't so gloomy. She had broken her first appointment with death. But underneath now she was set in what she wanted, and in what she believed was true.

At the beginning of 1914 she was in the room her friend had found for her, in an area on the edge of Chelsea called (she noticed) World's End. It was a depressing room, with an ugly, bare table. She saw some quill pens in a stationer's shop – red, blue, green and yellow: she bought them, to cheer up that damned table. When she noticed some exercise books she bought them too. After her supper of bread and cheese and a glass of milk, she suddenly felt her fingers and the palms of her hands begin to tingle, and she knew what she was going to do. She was going to write down everything that had happened: everything he'd said, everything she'd felt. She opened an exercise book and wrote, '*This is my diary.*'

For a week or ten days she wrote all day and far into the night, pacing her room, laughing and crying. Then it was finished, and the worst blackness lifted. She put the exercise books at the bottom of her suitcase and moved back to Bloomsbury. She knew now that when things got too bad, there was one thing she could do: write it all down. Then she could (almost) forget.

For the next eight or nine years, until she began writing stories and novels, she wrote in her diary whenever she was sad or excited, angry or hopeful. Later on she wrote *Voyage in the Dark* out of its first part. But she let the terrible years after the end of her affair, when she was young and alone in London, remain dark and forgotten. She hardly touched them in her fiction (only in *Till September Petronella*, set in the summer of 1914); she rarely spoke of them to anyone. But they taught her one of the dark, intensely experienced ideas that dominate her work: that life is a matter of animals fighting for survival, and if you let morality mean anything to you, you are trampled to death before you've begun.

Somehow, she survived. She made a little money sitting for artists; she went back briefly to the stage. But she mostly lived on Lancelot's allowance. During the war she worked for three days a week as a volunteer in a soldiers' canteen, serving the men bacon and eggs, coffee and sandwiches, before they left for France. The older ones were thoughtful and silent, she noticed; but the younger ones often looked excited. 'Close-up of human nature – isn't it worth something? . . .'

In the middle of 1917 her canteen closed. She was living in a cheap boarding house in Torrington Square, and there one afternoon she saw a new arrival. He was a slim man, with quick dark eyes; his name was Jean Lenglet. He was very different from Lancelot – not English, and not stiff and cautious either. He was much more like Ella herself: reckless and fun-loving, a middle-class rebel whose more reasoned dissent from 'respectable' society would help her to put her own feelings into words. He was half-French and half-Dutch; he was generous and romantic, direct and natural. Ella didn't fall in love with him but she liked him, and was impressed by him. She felt he liked women, and understood them; she felt he was contained and sure, and could take her away. When after only a few weeks he asked her to marry him, she accepted without hesitation.

She had to wait out 1918 before she could join him in Holland, and she took a job in a pensions office. But at the start of 1919 she wrote to Lancelot. With acute pleasure she told him that she would not need his money any more, because she was getting married. Lancelot asked to see her. 'I hate to say this,' he said, 'but I feel I have to. M. Lenglet is not a suitable person for you to marry.' 'You don't know anything about him,' Ella said. But, strangely he did. Lancelot had been made a CBE, for his service on several important wartime committees: the most powerful of these was the Contraband Committee, which directed the blockade of Europe ... Well, what *had* Jean been doing? After fighting at Verdun, he had been recruited into the Deuxiene Bureau; he was, in fact, a French secret agent. But none of this did Ella know. 'There are several things I can't tell you,' Lancelot said, 'but if you marry him you'll be taking a very big risk.' 'I like taking big risks,' Ella said. 'Didn't you know that?'

She had to leave most of her clothes behind, because she couldn't afford to pay the seamstress who was making them. But she sailed for Holland with a feeling of triumph and gratitude. It had taken over ten years – but she had escaped at last. She would never return to England. No matter what: *never*.

iv. *Marriage*

Ella and Jean were married in Holland early in 1919. They sold everything they could, and at last, in the summer, they arrived in Paris. Ella waited for Jean in a café while he went to meet friends. When at last she saw his face, she knew he had got some money. They went to a restaurant and ate ravioli. Ella thought, 'I've never been so happy in my life. I'm alive, eating ravioli and drinking wine. I've escaped.' She looked around her at Paris – its pink light, its feeling of freedom – and she felt, 'This is beautiful, this is grand, this is what I hoped for.'

They lived in a cheap hotel in the Rue Lamartine. Jean found a job, though he was vague about what it was; Ella supposed he didn't like it and preferred not to talk about it. She found a job too: and though Jean said she would never keep it, she did. She would have kept it forever, if she could: she was very happy.

Her job was to speak English to the grandchildren of the

Richelot family – and even *she* could speak English to children. The Richelots were an old, half-Jewish Parisian family. They were very rich, very civilized, and very kind. She loved them all; but especially she loved the daughter of her own age, Germaine. As soon as Ella saw her she knew that Germaine Richelot was even more timid, anxious and sensitive than herself: and immediately she became quite calm. Germaine was so kind, she gave everything away. She sat in her family's Daimler in an agony of discomfort, and told Ella how much she would rather be on a bus, or a tram. 'Or perhaps,' she would say shyly, 'a motor-bike – I would like that . . .' The Richelots' quiet, safe house enveloped Ella during the day; in the evening she returned to Jean, and the gaiety and pleasure of the cafés and terraces. 'Both sides of me were satisfied – the side which wanted to be protected, and the side which wanted adventure, strangeness, even risk.' She had no money, and no idea what they were going to do about the baby she was carrying. But sitting on a bench in the Champs-Elysées, watching her smallest charge riding around in a goat-cart, she was perfectly happy.

But that happiness ended abruptly. 'Life was like that. Here you are, it said, and then immediately afterwards, Where are you?' On 29 December her baby was born. It was a boy, and they called him William Owen. He was a beautiful baby – perhaps too beautiful? He lay quietly in his basket near the balcony – perhaps too quietly? One day the *sage femme* came and said he must go to hospital. As they had no money he was taken to the Hospice des Enfants Assistés, in the Rue Denfert Rochereau. To calm Ella's fears Jean fetched a friend, and two bottles of champagne, and they drank and drank until they had forgotten. When they received a message the next day, 20 January, to say that the baby had died of pneumonia the night before, Ella thought, 'He was dying while we were drinking champagne.'

Very soon after, Jean left Paris for a new job: secretary-interpreter with the Allied Commission in Vienna. The Richelots took care of Ella in the weeks before she could join him. Germaine took her to lunch, lent her money to buy clothes, lectured her, in her soft precise voice, on the evils of alcohol. She said good-bye to Ella with tears in her eyes, but Ella couldn't cry: once again she was seized with hope and excitement, and the need to leave unhappiness behind her.

She arrived in Vienna in the springtime, and Vienna always meant blue sky and the smell of lilacs to her. It meant lovely food, too – and lovely women, and lovely music, and the dread of poverty disappearing. For inflation was raging in Austria, and if you had foreign currency and were willing to take a risk, there was a lot of money to be made. Almost everyone they knew was making money out of the exchange, and Jean would too. He was a gambler by nature, and the war had thrown him very much on his own resources. He was determined that he and his wife – so passive and dependent, so easily despairing and so easily happy – would survive. They would not be poor any more; they would lose no more children. He would never cheat an individual, but governments, banks, huge and rich institutions – that was different. Again he offered no explanations to Ella, but in the spring of 1921 they moved into a smart hotel. It was the spending phase. They had a car, and a chauffeur; Ella had rings, flowers, compliments, dresses. A striped taffeta dress with velvet flowers tucked into the tight waistband, a white satin dress (the cheapest but the prettiest) and a black one, a white muslin dress and a blue one, a dirndl, a long blue and yellow dress like cornfields and the sky . . . Ella looked in the glass and thought: 'I've got what I wanted. I gambled when I married and I won.'

But she knew by now the treachery of fate, and she was worried. It would be harder now – it would be impossible – to be poor again with courage and dignity. She didn't want to work, she didn't want to wear ugly clothes. She was weak, weak, weak – but she didn't want to change.

The Commission moved to Budapest, which she thought even lovelier than Vienna. She found she was going to have another baby, and she was very pleased. She lay on the sofa, plunged in a dream of maternity. But not for long – her presentiments had been right. A man from the bank called, a fat man with a square, vengeful back. Looking at his back, she guessed everything. Finally, Jean admitted it: he had lost a lot of money on the 'change – other people's money, the Commission's money . . . He wanted to put a bullet in his head. But again Ella chose survival, however twisting and turning and mean. Her hands trembled with fright and cold, but at one o'clock in the morning they packed, and at six they slipped out of the hotel and drove away. 'Allons!' Jean said, with one of his sudden, resilient changes of mood. 'Allons! Au mauvais jeu il faut faire bonne mine.' But it was horrible to feel that henceforth she would live with the huge machine of law and order against her; horrible to feel she was not strong enough to fight it. They dodged across the endless plains of central Europe like hunted animals –

Prague – Warsaw – then Paris and London ... running away again, always running away.

v. *The End of Marriage*

By the end of 1922 Ella and Jean were back in Paris with their baby daughter, Maryvonne. They were back in the grip of poverty as well. Ella suggested that Jean write some articles, which she would translate and sell to one of the English papers. When the articles were ready, she put on the only pretty dress she had left from Vienna days and went to the offices of the *Continental Daily Mail.*

She did not sell the articles there, or anywhere – but they changed her life, as much as Myrtle's letter had, long ago. For after seeing her translations, Mrs George Adam, wife of *The Times* correspondent in Paris, asked if she had ever written anything herself. The next day Ella reluctantly left her diary with Mrs Adam's concierge (perhaps it would be forgotten, and 'that would be fate and have nothing to do with me').

Mrs Adam read the diary, and liked it. She tidied it up and edited it; she called the result *Suzy Tells*, and sent it to the novelist, critic and editor of the *transatlantic review*, Ford Madox Ford. Ford saw, underneath Mrs Adam's rather conventional and sentimental reworking, a natural and individual writer. He changed *Suzy Tells* to *Triple Sec*, and Ella Lenglet to Jean Rhys. He advised her and encouraged her; he told her to read the French classical writers, and to write about what she knew. When his advice agreed with her instincts as a writer, she followed it; otherwise, she didn't. For she had always had those instincts: in the poems and plays of her childhood; in the diary itself, parts of which she had stopped writing because they 'weren't good'. But now, with this large, clever, powerful man as her patron, she dared to think of herself as a writer. She had found 'the one thing she could do', and she began to do it. She was grateful to Ford, she admired him, she felt safe with him. When, in the autumn of 1923, the police at last found Jean and arrested him, it was inevitably Ford to whom she turned.

In *Quartet*, Jean Rhys's novel about her marriage, the heroine thinks that her husband is 'probably a bad lot' from the start, but she doesn't mind. He is 'so sure of himself, so definite'; he knows the clothes that are best for her and the life that is best for her. But when he is arrested and she sees him in prison, he is nervous and furtive. He has lost his faith in himself – and so, immediately, has she.

Jean Lenglet wrote his own novel, *Barred*, about these events, in which he called Ella 'Stania'. 'I have lost my prestige with Stania,' the hero says. 'If we were to stay for years together she would never be able to forget that she had seen me shiver when a warder spoke.' He knows that protection is what his wife needs, and that if he cannot give it to her she will have to find it somewhere else. Even so, Jean's pride was deeply wounded by Ella's strange passivity, her inability to defend herself and wait for him, like the other prisoners' wives aren't waiting for *him* . . . He loved her despite everything, for her charm, her 'manners of a great lady', her beauty, her generosity of spirit; but he could not forgive her betrayal of him. When he left prison and came face to face with it, their marriage was over.

As for Ella . . . what her husband wrote was true: 'After

one week of misery Stania would be lost to me.' She was like an alcoholic, who was so full of drink already that one small glass made her very drunk: those years alone in London, the flight across Europe – she was so full of fear and insecurity that one week alone plunged her into despair. And, in despair, how could she resist Ford, who looked so much the calm, blue-eyed English gentleman she always instinctively trusted? Nor could Ford resist her: for his greatest desire was to be that gentleman, and his greatest pleasure to play at being him – especially with childlike, submissive, mournful girls like Ella. Nine years before, in 1915, he had written *The Good Soldier*, a novel about an English gentleman whose wife accepts and even manages his love affairs, in order not to lose him. It was almost a blueprint for the terrible game of *Quartet*. Ella already believed in an ineluctable fate; and this time it really did seem to lie in wait for her, already decided and written down in Ford's book – as her last heroine Antoinette's fate had already been decided and written down in Charlotte Brontë's novel, *Jane Eyre*.

In *Quartet* the game is very simple: Heidler and his wife Lois – Ford and his common-law wife Stella Bowen – are cruel, invulnerable people; Marya and Stephan – Ella and Jean – are their natural victims, worn down by life, without a chance from the start. Marya feels she cannot help Stephan – she is wasting her life in impotent pity and despair: 'And her longing for joy, for any joy, for any pleasure, was a mad thing in her heart.' Heidler knows that she has a 'fear complex' and will be an easy prey. He says so, brutally: 'I knew that I could have you by putting my hand out . . . and now I know that somebody else will get you if I don't. You're that sort.'

Marya *is* that sort, and so was Ella: helpless and passive, disdaining consequences, pretending not to care. But of course she did care. That is why she first called her book *Postures* – because, she said, everyone was pretending. She was pretending to be reckless, but was really lonely and afraid; Stella was pretending to be 'a sport', but was really fighting her last battle to keep Ford (they parted in 1927); Ford was pretending to be in love with Ella, but was really only oiling his emotional and artistic machinery. It was a horrible game, in which everyone except Jean behaved very cruelly. Ella behaved as cruelly as anyone; but she was also by far the weakest. 'Let's go to Luna Park,' Lois Heidler says in *Quartet*. 'We'll put Mado on the joy wheel, and watch her being banged about a bit.' Ella was 'banged about' so much she broke. She did not love Ford, as she had loved Lancelot. But she was weaker now, more worn down and helpless; and to lose a calm, protective Englishman *again* was too much for her. And so she became obsessed by Ford. Need for him and hate for Stella possessed her, 'as utterly as the longing for water possesses someone who is dying of thirst'. She was in a bad way. 'Hard hit. All in. And a drunkard into the bargain . . .'

In the end, of course, she lost Ford, and she lost Jean too. Once again all that was left was loneliness, fear, drink, and no money, no money. Once again she had to meet a lover who was no longer her lover; to look into his cold, cautious, English eyes and ask for money. And once again she punished herself and him by letting men pick her up. 'Why not?' says Marya. 'What's it matter?' One of them put two enormous blue silk handkerchiefs around the electric light. 'I've often noticed,' he said, 'that women, for one reason or another . . .*Enfin.*'

At the end of *Quartet* Marya tells Stephan everything, and he wants to kill Heidler. But that is not what she needs from him – and suddenly he is her enemy too. She screams at him, all the vile words she can find to torment him, until he hits her. The novel ends with Stephan going off on the arm of another girl, leaving Marya lying crumpled up and still. Perhaps she is dead, perhaps she is only unconscious. She is certainly finished.

Ella began to write Marya's story in the autumn of 1925, almost before it was over, in a hotel off the Boulevard Montparnasse. She began it as she had begun her diary – as a record of facts and an outpouring of feelings. But she was a writer now, and slowly she turned it into a novel. Her anger and bitterness against Ford were still too fresh and strong; they unbalanced *Quartet*, and made it her most self-centred, vengeful book. But it is still extraordinarily good. With only a few short stories behind her, her mature style is already here, almost completely formed.

She had sworn she would never, under any circumstances, go back to England. But that was in 1919, and now it was 1927. She was an English writer, with an English publisher – for Cape had just published her first collection of stories, *The Left Bank*. So despite everything, she left Paris; she left Jean and Maryvonne where they had settled together, in Holland; and she went back to England, to try to sell *Quartet*. She was no longer just Gwen Williams or Ella Lenglet, who was baffled and tormented by life; she was also Jean Rhys, who was determined to understand why.

CHAPTER THREE

Good Morning, Midnight: 1927–39

i. *Leslie*

Back in London, Jean – as she was known from now on –
took *Postures* to a literary agent whom Ford had found for
her. His name was Leslie Tilden Smith. The novel was hard
to place, because publishers were afraid it libelled Ford. But
Leslie persisted, and in 1928 it was published.

Now Jean's life changed completely. Until 1923 she had
written only 'in spurts', and for herself. By 1928 she had
two books to her name: not popular successes, but recognized by critics from the start as strikingly original and
truthful, with a lucid, bitter style. She no longer threw
herself into experience with the 'calculated recklessness' that
had tormented Jean Lenglet. Instead she withdrew from it
more and more, to write. Between 1928 and 1939 she
produced most of her life's work. She wrote and published
After Leaving Mr Mackenzie, *Voyage in the Dark* and *Good
Morning, Midnight*; she wrote many of the stories of her
second collection, *Tigers are Better Looking*; she wrote a series
of autobiographical reminiscences, on which she later drew

for novels and stories. The key to this transformation of her life into that of a writer was Leslie Tilden Smith.

Jean had originally meant to return to Paris as soon as possible. But she and Leslie began a '50–50 affair'; soon they were living together, and finally they married. They liked each other; they weren't in love. Leslie – Jean felt – never stopped loving his first wife, and she was never in love with anyone but Lancelot. But Leslie was, like Lancelot, an English gentleman. Alas, he was not as rich or as well connected, and he had chosen the uncertain, half-Bohemian life of a literary businessman. But he was well educated and well spoken, kind and chivalrous, reserved and self-controlled. In many ways he combined for Jean the best qualities of her other English gentlemen: Lancelot's kindness and sense of honour, and Ford's care for her writing.

The combination was unique in her life. She was not happy: that was no longer possible. They were always poor, and she longed for comfort and beauty; she desperately missed Maryvonne, who was growing up with her father in Holland and only came to England in the summers. Her past tormented her so that she had to write about it, and then writing tormented her: she had to drink to write, and she had to drink to live. But Leslie helped her more than drink. He borrowed money to send her to Paris, where she worked best. Then, once she was working, he helped her to stop. For she wrote and rewrote, in an obsessive search for perfection that would not allow her to let anything go. When Leslie knew that a manuscript was finished, he simply took it away from her. There would be a terrible row, but at least it was done; and soon Jean would forget her anguish and feel relieved. Then Leslie would edit, type and sell it, and handle her contracts and her money. He was not a successful businessman – he soon had to give up his agency and go back to being a publisher's reader. But Jean's books were not likely to make very much money anyway, and she did not expect them to. The main thing was that she didn't have to worry about business, or money, which always sent her into a spiral of panic and incomprehension. She didn't even have to worry about the daily domestic routine. She hated routine, and had too little patience and energy for housework. When she saw the gap between what she could make of their homes and what she would have liked, the little energy she had would drain away. She could cook well when she was 'a bit tight'; but left to herself she lived on bread and cheese. So Leslie did most of the cooking and cleaning and washing too.

At last, therefore, someone was taking care of her: rarely in comfort and never in security, but taking complete care of her. That is why she could write. *And yet she never wrote about anyone taking care of her.* Kind Leslie, who was always there, hardly entered the world she wrote about. He had come too late. Instead, she went over and over the loss of love, the loss of hope. Poor Leslie must have known, as he read and typed, that he could not restore them to her.

Nonetheless, from now on her work began to grow: she began to pursue her goal – to understand her life, and especially her suffering – with a new rigour and a new honesty. In *The Left Bank* and *Quartet* she had blamed the man, the world – everyone but herself – for the heroine's troubles. Starting with *After Leaving Mr Mackenzie* she began to detach herself painfully from her heroine. This was her greatest battle, and led her to the final answer to her question, 'Why do I suffer?' She fought the battle, and found the answer, alone, at her writing table; but she owed much to Leslie's help, and perhaps also to his benign influence on her view of the world.

ii. *After Leaving Mr Mackenzie*

After Leaving Mr Mackenzie is a turning point in Jean's work. In it Julia does not just suffer, as Anna and Marya did: she tries to understand her suffering. She is obsessed with the feeling that there is some terrible truth 'behind all this talking and posturing, and that the talking and the posturing were there to prevent her from seeing it':

... she was tortured because her brain was making a huge effort to grapple with nothingness. And the effort hurt; yet it was almost successful. In a minute she would know.

Julia never does know what this 'nothingness' is. But Jean was starting to understand: a pattern was emerging. In *Voyage in the Dark* Anna loses love, in *Quartet* Marya substitutes hate. In *Mackenzie* Julia is empty and indifferent; in *Good Morning, Midnight* Sasha has a last chance to regain love, and loses it. In *Wide Sargasso Sea* the idea of nothingness returns, and echoes through the novel like a lament. *There is no love*, at least for the heroine: there is only 'nothing' – emptiness, and the escape of death. That has become Jean's central, recurrent theme.

After Leaving Mr Mackenzie is thus a turning point in Jean's understanding of her fate; it is also a turning point in her understanding of herself. It sets Julia in several different relationships: with her mother and her sister Norah, with her ex-lovers Neil James and Mr Mackenzie, with her new half-hearted lover, George Horsfield. And in each of these relationships Jean turns her most uncompromising gaze upon Julia herself. Norah, Mackenzie, Neil James, all show Julia envy, hate and incomprehension – but she also shows envy, hate and incomprehension towards them. Jean sees clearly that Julia is irrational and irresponsible, melancholic, self-destructive, subject to fits of unfair, uncontrollable rage. She lets us see that Julia takes money without thanks, that she hardly recognizes the men she depends on as human, that she is consumed with hatred, that she is 'going dippy, I suppose'. She still sees things from Julia's point of view – that is her job, the thing that she and only she can do. But she can see beyond it too. She can see that Norah's life is just as hard and sad as Julia's, and that she is a victim too – 'middle class, no money'. And she can see that her lovers' cruelty and caution come not from invulnerability, like Heidler's, but from their own inadequacy and fear. She can see this especially about George Horsfield, who has a good deal of Leslie in him. She sees it less about Neil James and Mr Mackenzie, who are both based on Lancelot. Mackenzie is cold and cautious; a 'kink in his nature' attracts him to unhappiness, but 'when it came to getting out of these affairs his business instincts came to his help, and he got out undamaged'. Neil James says to Julia, 'I've got loads of time – heaps of time. Nearly three-quarters of an hour . . .'; finally he writes that he is sending her some money, 'because I want you to have a rest and a holiday, but I am afraid that after this I can do no more'. Jean had gone back to Lancelot for help at least once, when Maryvonne was born in 1922, and perhaps more often; and Neil James's feeling that 'everybody tried to get money out of him' was certainly Lancelot's when he was old. It is all too likely that Jean did go back to him again in the late 1920s, and that Lancelot said to her then things very like those that Mackenzie and Neil James say to Julia. That would hurt too much for detachment; it would keep alive her anger. Despite all Lancelot's kindness, therefore, the English gentleman who had been her greatest love became her worst enemy, and the last person she could forgive.

iii. *Voyage in the Dark*

That is one reason, perhaps, why Walter Jeffries in *Voyage in the Dark* is duller and less sensitive than Lancelot had been in 1910 – because Lancelot had made himself duller and less sensitive, the last time (or times) that Jean had seen him, before she wrote the book. For *Voyage in the Dark* was the novel she turned to now, in the early 1930s. Ford had said about the notebooks of her first diary, 'You'll need those. Don't tear them up or anything silly like that', and she hadn't. She took them out now, and began to write.

The end of her first affair was the saddest thing in her life; still, writing *Voyage in the Dark* was easier than usual. Going back so far – twenty years for the affair, and even more for her memories of childhood – gave her the relief of distance; but it was more than that. *Voyage in the Dark* released her from the worst terrors of adult self-knowledge, which she had begun to pursue before it, in *Mackenzie*, and would go on pursuing after it again. Anna Morgan is still young and pretty; she doesn't drink, or make scenes, or hate anyone. She is a victim of other people – as Marya is, in *Quartet*; but she is not yet as bitter and angry as Marya. She is an innocent victim: of Walter, who is weak and cowardly; of Vincent, who is a smug and smiling villain; of Hester and Ethel and Carl. Surely that is why *Voyage in the Dark* came easily – at least, more easily than the others; and why it always remained Jean's favourite among her novels. It is a lovely book – sad and funny, simple and yet complex; written 'almost entirely in words of one syllable', as Jean said, yet richly interweaving past and present, reality and dream. It is a perfect novel, but a small one; and perfect and small for the same reason – that in it Jean reduced the task she set herself, to learn the whole truth about herself and her suffering. *Voyage in the Dark* is only half the truth, the half that said things were other people's fault. It is therefore only a sad novel, and not a painfully angry one – for Jean's real anger was reserved for herself. And so it is perhaps her most charming novel, and the easiest one to read: but it is not her best or most important. She was at the peak of her powers as a writer, and it was as good as it could be without being wholly true. For that rare combination of greatest skill with greatest truth we have to wait for *Good Morning, Midnight* and *Wide Sargasso Sea*.

iv. *Towards Midnight*

Voyage in the Dark came more easily to Jean than the others, but it did not come easily. Nothing did any more. She 'had the horrors about it and about everything for a bit'; during its writing she sometimes drank two bottles of wine a day. As always, she had great trouble finding an ending – and when she finally found one, the publisher made her change it. She spent several dismal weeks over those last four lines, and felt ever after that they had been a mistake and a betrayal. *Voyage in the Dark* came out in 1934; it was well received, but her pleasure in it was spoiled. That was to be the pattern with her books from now on.

Around 1934, too, Leslie's father died. He had disapproved of Jean and of their liaison; his death, and the money he left Leslie, meant that they could marry. Jean was far too Edwardian to have enjoyed 'living in sin', and she was delighted. 'I was over forty when he asked me to marry him,' she wrote. 'I was so happy I could scarcely believe it.' Perhaps this marriage – not so obviously a gamble as the first, but a gamble as all marriages must be, especially for her – perhaps this would be the lucky one. And for Jean the writer it was. But for Jean the woman it was the old story: 'Things went wrong. It wasn't as I thought it would be.'

At first, though, all was hope and excitement. They would have a holiday, in Dominica; they would move to a lovely flat in an elegant Chelsea square. Jean knew that going back to Dominica was dangerous, 'but I want it so much – I can't help risking it'. In early 1936 they went. Back on her island after nearly thirty years, Jean felt, for a few weeks, saner and safer than she had for a long time. But it couldn't last. She couldn't bear the heat; she couldn't bear the cockroaches – 'several years' steady drinking haven't made me calm about cockroaches'. She was one of the old whites, and Dominica belonged to the black people now. She felt unwelcome, even hated. People told her there were no roads to all the old remembered places, where she wanted to take Leslie. She couldn't believe them. Even after they were lost for two hours in a thick forest, she couldn't believe that the roads had all gone – even the biggest one, the Imperial Road, that the British had laid with such ceremony: gold lace, cocked hats, swords . . . Away from England, Jean felt herself become a defender of English roads. Without them the island would revert to forest and darkness.

She went to see her father's grave and found it neglected, covered with weeds. 'The Celtic cross which my mother had put up so proudly was knocked over . . . I sat and wept for the past.' She took, and kept, hundreds of photographs of Dominica; but it was no good. Her past seemed to be taken away from her. It was no longer here – and if not here, where? These people did not like her; they did not like the memory of her father. She felt more homeless than ever before.

In New York on their way home she went on a huge spending spree, but it didn't help. She drank more and more to keep going, and ended by having a terrible quarrel with one of her few friends, the American writer Evelyn Scott. When she and Leslie arrived back in England she was badly shaken, and Leslie's money was gone. He went straight to his family to borrow more. Some of them were beginning to refuse; but his sister Phyllis was a rich and generous woman. From then until Leslie died she paid his rent, and sent extra sums when he needed them.

Jean and Leslie went to their Chelsea flat, but even with Phyllis's help they could only stay for seven or eight months. That was sad, for Paulton Square was comfortable and attractive. Jean needed her home to be pretty, as much as she needed her own face and body to be; and much of the daily misery of her grown-up life centred on having to live in dull or mean or ugly places. Whenever she moved – and with both Leslie and her last husband, Max, she moved all the time – she would try to make her new home beautiful. She would paint the walls in soft Mediterranean colours; she would move the furniture around, and buy cheap glass ornaments in bright colours to cheer things up. But most places defeated her in the end, and went back to being cramped and dismal. Paulton Square didn't, and she was happier there. Eliot Bliss, a novelist and friend of Jean's during this time, remembers her at Paulton Square, looking much younger than her forty-seven years, slender but not thin, with white hair fashionably blued and pretty clothes. She seemed housewifely, even houseproud: 'She liked to have everything around her right.' There were sketches of her on the walls, and a mural by a friend; there was beautiful furniture, and 'lovely pale green satiny sheets'. Jean even cooked delicious West Indian meals, spicy and exotic ... Like so much else, Jean could do housewifely things well, when she was in better spirits; but when she was too poor, depressed, or drunk to do them well, she preferred not to do them at all. Then she would pretend to herself and to everyone else that she couldn't do them, and that she didn't care.

Paulton Square, then, was briefly a better time. At least one literary friend visited regularly; Jean even went to one or two literary parties, and thought Rosamond Lehmann 'not bad at all'. To Eliot Bliss, Jean and Leslie looked happy together, and Leslie spoke very fondly of Jean to her. Nonetheless, Jean's life was steadily darkening now. She drank so heavily that Eliot Bliss, trying to keep up with her, was always ill after their evenings together. And when she was drunk she flew into rages. As always, she understood herself better than anyone. 'Once I got going,' she said about one of these rages, 'old griefs and grievances overwhelmed me. I got the nightmare feeling of a scene which with slight variations had often happened – as it has, and I mixed it up with all the other scenes . . .' All these scenes were the same scene to her, all the people she raged at were one person. Eliot Bliss understood this, when it happened to her, and so would a few other friends in Jean's life; they could remember that, as they have all said, 'Except when she was drunk, Jean had a very sweet temperament.' But not everyone could be so detached and understanding: not 'respectable' people, who kept their distance from her more and more; and often, alas, not those who were closest to her. She was bent on self-destruction, and whoever was nearest her must be destroyed too. That began to happen now, in the late 1930s, with Leslie.

They were so poor – he hid her drink – he left her alone – he showed her work to people before it was finished . . .

Leslie's friends and children began to see him with black eyes and a scratched face. He made up gentlemanly stories about accidents; but to his daughter Phyllis he confessed that sometimes, in a rage, Jean would attack him. She tore up work he had typed; she threw his typewriter out of the window . . . Leslie would rarely shout back, and never hit her. 'Usually he did not answer me – just looked at me with his marble face . . . the hanging judge's face.' Then he would go out and pace Hampstead Heath or Primrose Hill. By the time the Second World War had broken out and he had rejoined the Air Force, his love for Jean was very battered. He never withdrew his care and protection; but he must have welcomed the necessity to leave this maddening, tortured woman for most of the day, and to throw himself into the ordinary and affable routine of service life.

Poor Leslie – and poor Jean. He was too much what half of her had wanted: an English gentleman. He was too polite and too pacific; he could not fight back, but only withdraw into what she hated most, a cold and silent disapproval. Perhaps too – especially after they were married – he was too secure. There was still a side of her that needed risk, that felt trapped and bored and (even worse) unworthy, with such an immovably decent and reliable man. What she so impossibly needed was permanent love, not permanent sufferance. And Leslie did not love her enough – no one could. He loved her work; but that didn't help, perhaps it even made things worse. She always felt happiest with people who didn't like, or didn't even know, her work – because then she could be sure they liked *her*. That had always been true; for example, with Germaine Richelot, whom she had loved, and who had loved her better than *Quartet*. But now it was stronger still. For more and more her work explored her own unlovableness. Those who knew and loved it, therefore, knew and approved an account of herself which, the moment she moved away from the painful lucidity of writing, she rejected in anger and tried to forget in drink. Perhaps she felt: If Leslie loves my books, he cannot love *me* . . . But *did* he love her books, anyway? She knew that her kind of writing had nothing to do with money (though God knows she needed money): she simply didn't connect the two. But he did; as her agent, it was his job to. And so, perhaps, he tried to make her writing a bit less bitter, a bit less nihilistic. Perhaps he tried to change her – and that was something she could never bear. When she was old she remembered his kindness and his support; but she remembered even more his telling her repeatedly that she would never sell. 'I wrote without hope,' she said.

By the end of the 1930s they were very much alone, except for visits from Leslie's grown-up daughter and Jean's young one. Their poverty, Jean's crippling shyness and erratic behaviour, Leslie's inability to overcome any of these things: these had isolated them from the literary world, and from any other. The early years, before their marriage, had been their best; and the novels of those years, *After Leaving Mr Mackenzie* and *Voyage in the Dark*, show it. Though nothing could make them less than pure Jean Rhys, compared to *Quartet*'s hot rage and *Good Morning, Midnight*'s cold despair, they are calmer and less bitter. The novelist David Plante, who came to know Jean well in her old age, said that when she was happy she could let herself be sad;

when she was unhappy, she could only be angry. In this way *Mackenzie*, in 1930, and especially *Voyage in the Dark*, in 1934, are only sad. But by the time Jean came to her next novel, even kind and decent Leslie had been unable to stop the hour moving on from dog to wolf.

v. *Good Morning, Midnight*

Good Morning, Midnight begins with the Paris street outside Sasha's latest room. It is 'what they call an impasse': she has come to the end of her voyage.

Ever since Anna Morgan came to London Jean had been haunted by the imagery of streets, full of tall dark houses, hostile to her. More and more her heroine withdraws from the dangerous street into rooms. Her career is measured by the move from rooms to nice rooms, up to 'the dizzying heights of the suite', back down to nice rooms and to rooms. Never mind – so long as it's a room. 'A room is a place where you hide from the wolves and that's all any room is.' But in *Good Morning, Midnight* the wolf comes into the room – for Sasha is the wolf herself. 'One day,' she says, 'the fierce wolf that walks by my side will spring on you and rip your abominable guts out. One day, one day . . .' The story of *Good Morning, Midnight* is the story of what happens to Sasha when she becomes that wolf.

A young man, René, picks her up, and she thinks: 'This is where I might be able to get some of my own back. You talk to them, you pretend to sympathize; then, just at the moment when they're not expecting it, you say "Go to

Jean Rhys's mother,
Minna Rees Williams

Jean's family home in
Roseau, Dominica

ALFRED SUTRO'S VERSION OF
MAURICE MAETERLINCK'S

Monna Vanna

(Licensed by the Lord Chamberlain)

▼

CAST

Guido Colonna *(Commander of the Pisan Garrison)* Mr. NORMAN McKINNEL

Marco Colonna   *(Guido's Father)*   Mr. J. FISHER-WHITE

Prinzivalli   *(General, in the Pay of Florence)*   Mr. LIONEL ATWILL

Borso   }
          (Guido's Lieutenants)   { Mr. MONTAGU LOVE
(By kind permission of Mr. Cyril Maude)
Torello   }
                       { Mr. HOWARD STURGE

Trivulzio *(Commissioner of the Florentine Republic)* Mr. IVAN BERLYN

Vedio   *(Secretary to Prinzivalli)*   Mr. NORMAN HARLE
(By kind permission of Mr. Oscar Asche and Miss Lily Brayton)

{ Mr. W. E. BELL

Guards   *(Attached to the Pisan Garrison)*   { Mr. ARTHUR WEBSTER

{ Mr. EDWARD CRAVEN

and

Giovanna   *(Monna Vanna)*   Miss CONSTANCE COLLIER

Citizens, Peasants, Ladies-in-Waiting, Guards, etc.

Messrs. WYNDHAM, CHAMBERLIN, DAVIES, MONTAGUE ROLFE, DUNN,
SHERIDAN, BIRTON, LLOYD, BECKET, RADFORD, DREW, WHITEHEAD,
FIELD, ROSS, CLARK, BROWN, MARTIN.

Misses JONES, DE CRESSE, GABAIN, HESILRIGE, GRAY, LE GALLIENNE,
McCARTHY, CREED, CONSTANCE, JOHNSON, DILLON, EVANS, DAVIES,
LYONS.

(Some of the above appear by permission of Mr. Asche and Miss Brayton)

The Play Produced by LEON M. LION.

1914 programme showing Jean in the chorus under her stage name, Gray

Lancelot Hugh Smith,
fifteen years before Jean
met him

Julian Martin Smith,
the model for Vincent

Jean and Germaine
Richelot in Paris

Jean in Vienna

Jean Lenglet, *c*. 1920

Jean Rhys's favourite
picture of her daughter
Maryvonne

Jean in her thirties

Leslie Tilden Smith

Max Hamer as a young
man

Jean in her eighties

hell".' That was just what had happened to Anna Morgan: 'It was when I wasn't expecting it to happen, you see – just when I wasn't expecting it.' And of course Sasha is a portrait of what Jean had been trying – and failing – to become, ever since the end of her first affair. In Francis Wyndham's words: 'Jean, who was a loving and generous person, made up her mind to be selfish and cold. But of course this willed transformation was never complete.' Sasha's plan to wreak vengeance on men leaves René unscathed, but destroys her utterly.

In *Good Morning, Midnight* Sasha fails to be a wolf to René, but Jean is a wolf to herself. In Sasha she mercilessly explores her worst fears and her real demons: age and ugliness, drunkenness and paranoia. 'She's getting to look old. She drinks,' Sasha's friend thinks; even her love for Paris is explained away – because the drink is better there. Her husband leaves her because she is passive and lazy; and after him 'There was more than one monsieur . . . One of every kind . . .' She is alienated from other people: 'What is she doing here, the stranger, the alien, the old one? . . . I have seen that in people's eyes all my life'; she is even more alienated from herself: 'The other – how do I know who the other is? She isn't me.' But 'the other' makes her rave against people; and the other makes her send René away. Deep down she knows that he is natural and sincere, and that she has lost her last chance – her very last chance – of love. 'I knew,' she says. 'I knew. That's why I cried.' He has not stolen her money: he has not stolen anything from her. *It is she who has stolen it from herself.*

In Sasha, therefore, for a great and terrible moment, Jean

65

GOOD MORNING, MIDNIGHT: 1927–39

recognizes what she could not admit about Anna or Marya, or even wholly about Julia: that her suffering is her own fault. And something else too: that she is not different from other people, even the worst and maddest of them. The worst and maddest in the novel is the travelling salesman, the *commis voyageur*, with his 'mean flickering eyes' and his 'high mad gabble'. And at the end, having lost 'love, youth, spring, happiness', Sasha accepts the *commis* as her lover. Thus she accepts into herself, as equal to herself, what is mean and contemptible and mad: 'I look straight into his eyes and despise another poor devil of a human being for the last time.'

It is an extraordinary effort of her will towards compassion, towards admitting her identity with even the most hopeless of the human race. But – like Sasha – under this strain she cracks. For the extreme awfulness of the *commis voyageur*, and the unbearable horror of that last scene, tell us what she really feels about such madness and meanness, and how little she can really bear to identify herself with them. Even in her writing she could only briefly give up the agonies of paranoia, because she found the agonies of self-knowledge worse still. She does it in *Good Morning, Midnight* – but at the last moment, in that last scene, she only half achieves it. Anything more than half would drive her mad for good. And that, of course, is what happens in *Wide Sargasso Sea* to Antoinette.

Not surprisingly, Jean's usual struggle over endings was a protracted agony with *Good Morning, Midnight*. She drank a bottle of wine in order to get any ending at all; then 'the Man in the Dressing Gown appeared from Heaven knows where to supply the inevitable end'. But she remained terribly worried about it. Finally Leslie stepped in and made the decision. 'It was sent off while I was asleep,' Jean still remembered, more than twenty-five years later. 'The argument was still going on when Michael Sadleir rang up to say he liked it.' For 'argument' we must certainly read 'blazing row'. Then she had 'an awful time of despair', when she tore up the picture Sasha buys in the novel, and 'also the book and my contract, I think . . .' In the novel, she understands her violence and her self-inflicted wounds; in life she could no longer change.

Good Morning, Midnight was published in 1939. It had many very good reviews, and could easily have brought Jean the recognition at fifty for which, in the event, she had to wait until she was seventy-six. But the eve of war was a bad time for such a painful, desperate book. It found few enough readers in English, and the French wouldn't have it at all. When war broke out it was immediately forgotten, and all her other novels with it.

Jean's gloom and anger deepened. But one day Leslie handed her his favourite novel to read: *Jane Eyre*. She had read it when she was young; now she read it again. And soon Leslie was telling his daughter, 'Jean has had the most marvellous idea for a book.' She was very excited about it, and started work straightaway. By late 1939, when Leslie joined up, she had finished at least half, and possibly the whole, of the first version of *Wide Sargasso Sea*. She called it, provisionally, *Le Revenant*: 'The Ghost'. Leslie's daughter Phyllis remembers that he typed out the draft before the war. She remembers something else, too: that in a fit of rage one day, Jean burned it. Leslie was never able to type it out again. Jean kept her handwitten manuscript, but lost most of it later, when she was moving 'from somewhere to somewhere else'; many years later she found 'two chapters (in another suitcase)', and used them for *Wide Sargasso Sea*. But she had to undergo much more suffering before she could create the final version of Antoinette.

CHAPTER FOUR

Temps Perdi: 1940–57

i. *War*

The idea of time ending, time not existing any more, is
Jean's metaphor for death in life: for the delirium, uncon-
sciousness, indifference, and finally madness that overtake
each of her heroines in turn. Of the end of *Voyage in the
Dark*, for instance, she wrote, 'There's no more time for
Anna', and of the end of *Good Morning, Midnight*, 'I wanted
Sasha to enter the No Time region'. Now *she* entered the
'No Time region', and applied the metaphor to herself: *temps
perdi*.

   She did so in an autobiographical story of that name,
which she wrote in the early part of the war. To the English
reader *temps perdi* suggests 'lost time'; in Creole patois, she
tells us, it means 'wasted time, lost labour'. And that was
the worst of it. Despite everything in her nature that held
her back, she had 'worked hard for a long time'; but *'à quoi
bon?'* The war 'smashed everything' she had achieved, 'And
how!' It was like life on her island. 'You are getting along
fine and then a hurricane comes, or a disease of the crops

that nobody can cure, and there you are ...' (She had known that for a long time: 'Life was like that. Here you are, it said, and then immediately afterwards, Where are you?' – that was *Quartet*, a whole quarter of a century before.)

There were other reasons, too. She did not know where Maryvonne and Jean were, or whether they were alive or dead. Just once, later on in the war, she heard indirectly that Maryvonne was safe; but apart from that she knew nothing for five years: 'for though I tried every way I couldn't get a letter through'. In fact, both Maryvonne and Jean were lucky to survive. They had been caught working for the Dutch resistance; Maryvonne had spent a short time in prison, and her father four years in a concentration camp.

Around 1940, then, Jean was depressed and worried: and for the first time in twenty years, she was alone again. She had come with Leslie to his air force station in Norfolk; but he was away all day, happily involved in a life she couldn't share.

So here she is, in *temps perdi*: all alone in a freezing war-time winter, in a village where her house – the people – the sky – even the trees – all wear a hypocrite's mask to hide their hate ... All the hard-won self-knowledge of *Good Morning, Midnight* has dropped away, and her paranoia has returned. It has returned with such redoubled force that much of her heroine's strange, shadowy individuality is seared away, and only the classic symptoms of paranoia remain. People steal from her, and laugh at her – not 'a good, hearty shout or curse, just this silent, sly, shy laugh-ter'. She cannot even take refuge in books, because 'Now I am almost as wary of books as I am of people. They are also capable of hurting you, pushing you into the limbo of the forgotten. They can tell lies – and vulgar trivial lies . . .' These are the things which will surround her from now on, when she is at her lowest: hatred and thieves, laughter and lies.

She tried to escape her 'solitary confinement' by going to see a friend, Peggy Kirkaldy. But it didn't work. She said to Peggy that she realized that 'my talk of myself, Ford, Paris, *Perversité*, myself, gramophone records, myself was irritating you. But I couldn't stop.' She always realized it, and she could never stop. As usual, she ended by flying into a rage. 'Oh Peggy,' she wrote, when she was back in Norfolk. 'I can't bear much more of my hideous life.'

Then something happened only a few miles away from her, which if she knew of it must have increased her misery still more. Her long-ago lover Lancelot had owned The Old Hall at Garboldisham, near Norwich, since 1935. Two days after Jean returned to Norfolk, on 23 March 1941, he died there, and was buried in the churchyard.

Lancelot was seventy when he died, and a very rich and successful man. *The Times* gave him a large obituary. Did Jean see it? *Had* she gone back to him again, perhaps even after the late 1920s, the period of Julia's meeting with Neil James? If she had, much would be explained. During the 1930s her bitterness against England had grown, until by her *temps perdi* it was a huge obsession, that never left her again. Lancelot had always been England to her – the best of England, and the core of her bitterness was against him. Perhaps the end of their affair, and his washing his hands of her just before *Mackenzie*, were enough to produce that bitterness. But in his sixties, in the 1930s, Lancelot grew richer, crustier, narrower and more tyrannical than before: if Jean did go back to him then, he would almost certainly have refused, without much ceremony, to help or even to see her. That would have destroyed her last illusion, and spoiled the memory of her dream ... We cannot know; but this comes close to the sort of thing she said, and the degree of bitterness she felt. If it did happen this way, and if she now knew that he was dead, she would be overwhelmed by terrible bitterness and regret. For a time now she did briefly cross a line between anguish and breakdown: Lancelot's death may have been a reason.

The wartime story called 'I Spy a Stranger' charts a breakdown. The heroine is called Laura; her story is told by the cousin with whom she has been staying, Mrs Hudson, to her sister, Mrs Trant. 'She hadn't been here a week before they started making remarks about her, poor Laura,' says Mrs Hudson. People call her 'the crazy old foreigner, that witch of Prague'; they say, 'That horrible creature should be shot.' Laura keeps a diary, full of her obsessions: people are insects and society a machine; the English hate women, especially women writers. She has a terrible row with the old man next door, because he has a dog called Brontë, and he kicks it.

... 'Here's Emily Brontë or my pet aversion,' he says, and then he pretends to kick it. It's only a joke. But Ricky's right; she has no sense of humour ...

The doctor refuses to certify her – 'She's been treated badly, from all I hear,' he says. But Laura agrees she needs a rest. She has hardly any money, and the only sanatorium she can afford is 'a large, ugly house with small windows, those on the top two floors barred'. 'She can come away if she wants to,' Mrs Hudson says. 'Can she, do you think?' asks Mrs Trant. 'Well, I suppose she can,' says Mrs Hudson. 'I must say the doctor there doesn't seem –'

We do not know if Jean went to such a sanatorium now, but it would not have been for the first or last time in her life. She certainly had some sort of breakdown in Norfolk. She was miserable and agitated and quarrelling with everyone. Leslie's job – like Ricky Hudson's – was in Intelligence; finally Jean's behaviour was so bad that he was considered a security risk and transferred away from Norfolk. Eventually he was posted back to London. There Jean went to work on a series of short stories, all of which explore Laura's obsessions like wounds.

Audrey, the heroine of 'The Insect World', sees people as insects; Inez, in 'Outside the Machine', sees them as parts of a machine, working smoothly and certainly:

Even if the machine got out of control, even if it went mad, they would still work in and out, just as they were told . . . She lay very still, so that nobody should know she was afraid. Because she was outside the machine they might come along any time with a pair of huge iron tongs and pick her up and put her on the rubbish heap, and there she would lie and rot. 'Useless, this one,' they would say.

The heroines of these wartime stories are only barely in control. Inez and Audrey rage at people; Teresa of 'A Solid House' laughs at all the wrong moments, with a laugh that 'came from the depths of her – a real devil of a laugh'. Teresa is the farthest along the road that 'leads to madness and death, they say': the road to Antoinette. She has been ill and in hospital; she has made a suicide attempt. She describes this state once more as an end of time, and its atmosphere of timeless, placeless dream exactly prefigures the last pages of *Wide Sargasso Sea*:

> I went upstairs and put on my blue dress and powdered my face. I didn't hurry, but when I came down again the hands of the clock hadn't moved at all. Which shows that it's true, what they say: 'Time is made for slaves'. Then I knew I must do it and so I swallowed all the tablets in the bottle with the whisky . . . When I woke up the first thing I saw was the blue dress on the chair. And the doctor was there . . . So I knew it was Tuesday. A whole night and a day gone, and I shall never know what happened. And afterwards too I don't remember. I had dreams, of course. But were they dreams?

Jean worked on these stories very hard, to turn them, as she turned her novels, from raw emotion into literature. But the emotions of her *temps perdi* were too raw, too close to breakdown and delusion. Her notebooks and drafts for the stories show how close they were. They are wild, obsessive, almost illegible, plunged into a pit of hatred for England: 'Rot its mean soul of shit.' Jean felt she had worked on them *too* hard – 'so afraid of offending that I wrote and rewrote the life out of the things'; but they still remained, she knew, 'too bitter'. In 1945 she put them together with several other stories and tried to sell them, but she failed. When the collection, *Tigers are Better Looking*, was finally published in 1968, 'Temps Perdi' and 'I Spy a Stranger' were left out, and printed separately.

The failure of these wartime stories is very revealing. For stylistically they are as perfect as the rest of her work: style,

therefore, was not enough. What she had always to fight for
in her work was what she had to fight for in life, too: the
control of her demons, self-pity and paranoia; and a recognition of the reality, and the vulnerability, of other
people. That is what she had achieved in *Mackenzie* and
Good Morning, Midnight; and what, after a long dark night
of her soul, she would achieve again in *Wide Sargasso Sea*.

ii. *The Sound of the River*

By 1944 Leslie had rejoined Jean in London. She was so low
now that he asked even his daughter not to visit them. She
was troubled by illness, forebodings, dreams. 'I grew frightened of my own loneliness,' she wrote, 'and the strain
smashed me up sometimes.'

As soon as Leslie was demobbed, in August 1945, he
went to his sister and borrowed enough money to take Jean
on a holiday. They found an isolated cottage on Dartmoor,
and hid themselves away to recover and rest.

But it was too late – Jean's despair had exhausted them
both. Her own frailty hid an extraordinary tenacity; but
Leslie was not so strong. Everyone had forgotten that his
First World War medical tests had shown up a slight heart
weakness; he didn't think of it himself, even when he began
to have pains in his chest and arm. But on the morning of 2
October he was suddenly in such pain that Jean had to run
and fetch help. It was all 'slow and slow as a nightmare',
and they were still alone in the cottage when Leslie died.

In her stories, Jean had already given one name to what

she feared: hate. Now she gave it another: death. She feared hate because it annihilated her, she feared annihilation for itself. Now it had come very close, and taken Leslie from her. The experience was so terrible that she had to write about it almost straightaway. She called the story 'The Sound of the River'. In it, an unnamed man and woman lie in bed in a cottage near a river, and she tells him she is afraid.

'All the time?'
'Nearly all the time.'
'My dear, really. You are an idiot.'

Not about this, she thinks. And when she wakes up in the morning and touches his hand, he is dead. The doctor comes and questions her suspiciously: why did it take her so long to fetch help? It was, she thinks, because she *knew*:

I was late because I had to stay there listening. I heard it then. It got louder and closer and it was in the room with me. I heard the sound of the river.
I heard the sound of the river.

Someone phoned her brother Edward, a Colonel in the Indian Medical Service only recently retired to England. He came, paid for the cottage, and took Jean to his home in Devon. Maryvonne, too, came from Holland and stayed with her. Leslie was cremated at Plymouth, and his ashes taken to London, to be buried beside those of his parents.

Jean couldn't face the funeral in London, but she went with Edward to the cremation. She wrote to Leslie's daughter, Phyllis Smyser:

... It was a fine and clear day and I had all the time the feeling that Leslie had *escaped* – from me, from everyone and was free at last ...

I shall not ever forgive myself that I didn't stand up to things better – not ever ... I did love him though and knew all his generosity and gentleness – very well.

iii. *Max*

Jean's brother Edward and his wife 'are terrified poor dears that I will sit down on them for good', Jean wrote to Peggy Kirkaldy, and as soon as she could she went back to the flat she had shared with Leslie. But from now on she longed to leave London and live in the country. 'I've a *horror* of London,' she told Peggy, 'I will go to pieces there alone ... If you know of a nice cottage (no rats) will you tell me? ... I'd like to spend my last months in the country.'

From now on, too, she wanted above all to finish her novel: 'partly because Leslie liked it, partly because I think it might be the one book I've written that's much use'. But her troubles were more pressing than ever. Leslie had left her penniless, and his sister had stopped paying the rent when he died. Jean wrote to Peggy, 'As I don't play cards I figure the balloon will go up in about six months.'

But the balloon did not go up; as always, she hung on and survived – only to think afterwards that it would have been better if she had given up. As always, too, she survived because someone came and rescued her. 'Saved, rescued, fished-up, half-drowned, out of the deep, dark river', as she had written in *Good Morning, Midnight.* 'Nobody would know I had ever been in it. Except, of course, that there always remains something . . .'

She was rescued by Leslie's cousin, Max Hamer. They had met during the war, and already then Max had admired her. They met again now because Max was the executor of Leslie's will. Jean was fifty-five, Max sixty-three; he was married, with a grown-up daughter. He was rather like Leslie, though smaller: slight, gentle and blue-eyed. He came from a naval family, and had been a lieutenant commander during the war; now he was working as a solicitor. This time Jean did not have to live in sin for several years: Max got his divorce quickly, and they were married in 1947.

Jean's 'seven years' bad luck' should have been over. Leslie had always kept a part of himself separate from her – because of his love for his first wife, or just because he was a reserved and diffident man. Jean Lenglet too, in his proud, mercurial way, had been an independent and elusive person. Max Hamer was the one who loved Jean most unreservedly and unmistakably, so that even she must have felt – at least sometimes – secure in his love. She often said, in old age, that this third marriage was her happiest one, and that was probably why. But it could not really be happy. Much as Max loved her, he was not the right person to rescue her from the river, or to keep her dry. He was naïve and unworldly, an enthusiast, even a fantasist. He was full of get-rich-quick schemes: inventions of his own, ideas for investing in other people's.

'Max is a very optimistic man,' Jean wrote early on in their marriage. 'He always has some music hall act or another which he imagines will get rid of all the sea of troubles.' Instead, he only plunged deeper. They moved into a large, decaying house at Beckenham, in Kent, and Max employed some builders to do the repairs cheaply, on the black market: they absconded with his money. That was the sort of thing that kept happening. He was an intelligent, generous and sweet-natured man, but he was even more incompetent than Jean about money. And that meant disaster for both of them. Instead of her worst time being over when she married Max, it was only just beginning.

iv. *Let Them Call It Jazz*

In the summer of 1948 Maryvonne came to visit Jean in Beckenham. She had seen her mother only three or four times since the war; in the meantime she had married and had a baby. Jean had been longing to see her, and the new granddaughter she had never met. Yet when Maryvonne arrived everything was in chaos: there was no food in the house, nothing for the baby, not even a cup of tea. Jean was in a deep pit of depression, drinking heavily and hardly eating at all.

The reasons were the same as ever: poverty, fear and loneliness. She was alone most of the time. Max was in the City, with his increasingly unreliable, even dangerous, friends. By Christmas, she was in a frenzy of anxiety. She and Max began to quarrel constantly and loudly. The paranoia and paralysis of her lowest moments began to appear: the neighbours gossiped about her; their dogs killed her cats; her cellar filled up with rats . . . She couldn't write; she was haunted by the fear that she would never finish her novel. In the spring of 1949 she cracked. 'I didn't drink so much but I didn't eat much either and was desperate inside. One day the man in the flat upstairs was rude to me. I slapped his face. He had me up for assault.' She had quarrelled with this man, and his wife, before. He had probably shown that he despised her – years later he still wrote contemptuous letters to her publisher – and she had responded by focusing her hate on him. She railed at both of them, she said unforgivable things, she banged her fists on their door . . . On 6 May 1949, she was found guilty of assault; at the end of June she was remanded in custody and sent to the hospital wing of Holloway Prison. She spent only five days there. The doctors pronounced her sane; she was put on probation for two years and allowed home.

Straightaway she began to write a story, 'Let Them Call It Jazz', which took ten years to finish. It is about a black woman, Selina Davis, who is sent to Holloway – because, as she says, 'if they treat you wrong over and over again the hour strike when you burst out'. In Holloway she feels 'it all dry up and hard in me now', until she hears a woman singing the Holloway song 'high up, from one of the small barred windows'. The song means 'cheerio and never say die', and it restores Selina to freedom. Even when she loses it to a man who jazzes it up and sells it, she thinks, 'So let them call it jazz . . . That won't make no difference to the song I heard.'

Once before, in *Good Morning, Midnight*, Jean had told the story of a black woman, so rejected and despised that she is 'no longer quite human, no longer quite alive'. Whenever she was hurled most low, Jean found a black woman from her islands to speak for her; and in her she found once again courage and dignity, strength and even humour. It would happen again in *Wide Sargasso Sea*, when Antoinette feels identity with Tia, and finds comfort and alliance in Christophine.

When she was home from Holloway Jean wrote bravely and gaily to Maryvonne, saying only that she had been ill and in hospital. 'Max sends his love too,' she wrote. 'He has discovered *another* friend who is promising heaven and earth but I have grown so cautious!' Max's new friend was called Michael Donn. He already had two convictions for fraud and black market activities, and when Max met him he had only recently come out of prison. Jean wrote to Peggy: 'I saw at once that he was up a different street.' She tried to warn Max; but he was an obstinate man and, it seemed, mesmerized by Donn. Every night he sent Jean a wire to say he was 'detained'; every day he said 'Tonight Donn's getting me two hundred or five hundred', and got 'more haggard and shabby and disappointed'. He told Jean that he and Donn had left the solicitors they had been working for, Cohen & Cohen, and were going to set up on their own: 'He said they'd make all the money in the world because Donn knew all the crooks in London. (That part I believed.)'

By the beginning of 1950 Jean was drinking so much and eating so little that her hands shook uncontrollably and she slept 'all the time', as she had done in the weeks after the end of her first affair. Towards the end of January Max disappeared. A few days later she heard the news: he and Donn had been arrested. In February it was in the papers:

A charge of stealing seven cheque forms, valued at 1s.2d., was made at Guildhall yesterday against George Hamer, 67, solicitor of Southend Road, Beckenham, Kent, and Michael Donn, 35, solicitor's managing clerk, of Ellingford Road, Hackney.

Another nightmare of accusation and judgement had begun.

After several committal proceedings and postponements, Max's trial was set to begin at the Old Bailey in May. Jean wrote to Peggy: 'Poor little Max, he is so smashed up and I cannot comfort him at all.' She alternated between blankness and thoughts of suicide; but she arranged to sell everything they owned, and went over and over the old question: '*What* to do, *what* to do?' She couldn't type; she was too slow and lethargic to be a servant. 'I could read to people,' she wrote pathetically to Peggy. 'I know a woman in New York who used to earn a sort of living that way . . .' They moved up to London for the trial and lived for a while on the money from their sale. Then once again Jean seemed almost magically to draw the means of survival towards her, by her helplessness and need: 'A friend who wishes to remain anonymous will supply me with money to live on for the present. I don't know who it is.' Max thought it was Lord Listowel, who was a relative; Phyllis Smyser thinks it was Leslie's sister once more, who was also a cousin of Max's. Jean was certain it was no member of her own family. Her belief in fate and magic was confirmed: whenever she was about to go under, something came to save her – if only to make a figure of fun out of her, as she had written in *Good Morning, Midnight*, long ago.

On 9 May Max's trial began. He and Donn were charged with stealing cheques worth up to £1500, and with fraudulently obtaining sums of money from clients of Cohen & Cohen. Max confessed to two counts and Donn to four. Max was sentenced to three years (Donn got four), and was sent to Maidstone Prison.

Jean wrote to Maryvonne, saying only that Max 'got into money difficulties but I think all will be well now'. She moved down to Maidstone to be near him.

Max earned full remission of his sentence, but he still spent two whole years in prison, until June 1952. God knows how either of them survived. The first year, up to the spring of 1951 – while Jean was still on probation for her own offence – has dropped almost completely out of her life. She wrote few letters to anyone; she told no one the real situation. On 25 May 1951, Max's name was struck off the Solicitors' Roll. In his prison cell he still thought of Jean, saving his ration coupons for her. Had he done it all for her? Was there something about Jean – the power of her need for comfort and glamour – that drove her husbands to obtain for her by fraud what they could not obtain any other way? Even she was struck by the way two of her three husbands ended up in jail – 'Funny,' she mused, about Jean Lenglet, 'he was odd about money too . . .' Jean Lenglet and Max were both natural gamblers; but they were also well-educated middle-class men and the force of Jean's need drove them further than they would have gone without her. War and statelessness, as well as his young wife's dependence, had made Jean Lenglet an adventurer, with a romantic code of panache and honour among outcasts; but until he married Jean, Max had remained an unremarkable member of his respectable military and professional family. He had the hidden streak of difference which marked out the Englishmen, from Lancelot onwards, whom Jean had drawn towards her. But now he had gone far out of his depth. Once again Jean was the stronger: 'I am the cat with nine lives,' she said. Max lived another fourteen years after he left prison, but he was never really well again.

v. *The Ropemakers' Arms*

This last 'smash' was so bad that Jean couldn't even write. Ever since she had seen it coming she had been unable to write: 'The desire has gone . . . It's the first time in my life (my life since I can remember) that it's happened,' she told Peggy, in October 1949. Her brain was like an automatic dispenser she had seen in the Tube: 'This machine is EMPTY till further notice.' From 1949 until 1951, for the first time in her adult life, she almost certainly wrote nothing at all. When she did, it was to return to the very first form she had used, to lift the blackness of her first big 'smash': a diary.

She began this new diary towards the end of 1951, in a pub near Maidstone called the Ropemakers' Arms. The part of it she kept (for later she tore out most of its pages) was published after she died in her autobiography, *Smile Please*.

Its first line is 'Death before the Fact': she was, in all important ways, dead already.

That was an old theme of hers – that she had really died at the end of her first affair, and died again many times since, each time a bit more. And now that we know more of her sufferings, however self-inflicted, can we say – as people usually did – that she exaggerated? It was an extraordinary triumph of her will to live and to make something of her life that she wrote the Ropemakers' diary at all, in the first moment of peace that she could find. But *what* she wrote was even more extraordinary. For in the Ropemakers' diary she seems to have returned, with more honesty and clarity than ever, to the pursuit of true, unsparing self-knowledge that she had left off in 1939. It was as though the real horrors of Leslie's death and Max's disaster had burnt away the terrible but comforting delusions of the war and the wartime stories, and she could start again.

The Ropemakers' diary is not really a diary at all, but, for most of its fourteen pages, a drama. Its form comes straight out of Jean's experience of the last two years: it is a trial. There is the Counsel for the Prosecution, the Counsel for the Defence, and the accused, who is unnamed except in the title: *The Trial of Jean Rhys*. The accused offers only one excuse: 'I learnt everything too late.' The rest is a confession. Did she try to make contact with other people – friendships, love affairs, and so on?

Yes. Not friendships very much.
Did you succeed?
Sometimes. For a time.
It didn't last?

No.
Whose fault was that?
Mine I suppose.

She admits that her hatred for England is 'disappointed love', she admits that she has been accused of madness. And she admits that everything, *the worst as well as the best*, is in her: 'Good, evil, love, hate, life, death, beauty, ugliness ...' 'Oh, God, let me be pretty when I grow up,' she had prayed when she was a little girl; but now she accepts that she is ugly too. She is guilty of 'pride, anger, lust, drunkenness??, despair, presumption (hubris), sloth, selfishness, vanity ...' Her only good, the only thing that she can do, is write. 'If I stop writing my life will have been an abject failure. It is that already to other people. But it could be an abject failure to myself. I will not have earned death.' So she must go on writing.

This is the way?
I think so.
All right, but be damned careful not to leave this book about.

vi. *Selma*

In early May 1952 Max was released from prison, and they returned to London. Jean was sixty-two; Max was nearly seventy. Their poverty was terrible. Max could no longer work as a solicitor, and now the Navy took away his pension too; the unknown donor's help could not go on forever. They would take nothing from Maryvonne and her husband, Job, who were struggling to build a life in Indonesia; they would not even tell them. Maryvonne believes that their main help now came from Jean's brother, Edward: and many years later David Plante found, in the margins of pages torn from the Ropemakers' diary, bits of what look like drafts of a letter to Edward about money. It was probably with his help, therefore, that they now survived.

During the next few years, Jean clung to two hopes: to leave London, and to get back to her novel. The two were connected, for in order to write she needed peace, and 'a room of my own'. At the end of 1952 Max wrote most pathetically to Oliver Stoner (the novelist Morchard Bishop), who had corresponded with Jean after *Good Morning, Midnight*, and who later became a good friend of hers in Devon. 'My wife Jean Rhys,' Max wrote, 'has had a very difficult time since her husband died and now is most anxious to resume what she feels is the only career she is fit for i.e. Writing. My own bumbling efforts have proved quite fruitless so I thought of writing to you to ask if you have any suggestions to make. Our present difficulty is accommodation and I thought that possibly you might know of somewhere in the West Country where it would be possible to rent a cottage.'

Several efforts came to nothing. In 1953 they escaped briefly to Wales; but soon they were back again, moving restlessly from room to room – Jean losing clothes, books, rings, manuscripts each time. Finally, in 1956, they got away. The cottage they had taken, sight unseen, at Bude in Cornwall turned out to be only a summer house, and desperately cold. But they had escaped London, with its crowds and noise, and its cruelty if you were poor. Jean and Max had been so poor that for the last two Christmases friends and relatives had sent them food.

In Bude they moved four times in search of that elusive peace, and warmth, and – if possible – a few trees. 'Sometimes there are lovely days,' Jean wrote to Maryvonne. 'There are wide lonely sands – and sunsets with fantastic clouds . . . So at moments I feel ashamed of disliking it here, only a little more and I would like it.' And finally her luck did change. In early October 1956 a friend told her that there was an advertisement in the *New Statesman*:

Would Jean Rhys or anyone who knows her whereabouts please get in touch with Sasha Moorsom, Features Department, BBC, in connection with a future Third Programme broadcast of *Good Morning, Midnight*.

Jean knew straightaway who was behind this renewal of hope for her – for it had happened, in almost exactly the same way, once before. In November 1949, just as Max's disaster was about to break over them, she had seen another advertisement in the *Statesman* for 'Jean Rhys (Mrs Tilden Smith), author of *Voyage in the Dark*, *After Leaving Mr Mackenzie*, *Good Morning, Midnight*, etc.'. It had been placed by an actress called Selma Vaz Dias, who had adapted *Good Morning, Midnight* into a monologue for radio, and wanted Jean's permission to perform it. Jean gave her permission; she met and corresponded with Selma; hope and excitement briefly lifted her out of her paralysis and despair over Max. But not for long. When Selma gave a preliminary reading of her monologue at an arts centre in London, Jean had been too depressed and ill to go. In the end the BBC had turned down *Good Morning, Midnight,* and slowly Jean had sunk out of sight beneath the waves of Max's smash.

Now, seven years later, she wrote to Selma – and it *was* her project which was being revived. So for a second time Selma brought Jean back to life – for again, of course, 'lost hope was the real trouble'. But this time there was a difference: *Good Morning, Midnight* would be performed. The flame of hope shot up once more, but this time it did not sink down again, 'useless, having reached nothing'. Jean wrote to Maryvonne: 'Just in time. I was nearly done.'

CHAPTER FIVE

Wide Sargasso Sea: 1957–66 – and Back to 1890

i. *The Writing of* Wide Sargasso Sea

Good Morning, Midnight was performed on the Third Programme on Friday 10 May and Saturday 11 May 1957. In the *Radio Times* the week before Selma had published an article called 'In Quest of a Missing Author'. This brought Jean a letter from the man who was to become, after Ford Madox Ford and Leslie Tilden Smith, her third great literary support and mentor: Francis Wyndham.

In 1957 Francis was working as an editor with the publishing firm of André Deutsch. He had discovered Jean's novels during the war, with a shock of pleasure and amazement. Like everyone else, he had thought that Jean was dead. Now he was overjoyed to learn that this was not true, and he asked if she was still writing. She had been writing – or at least, had been longing to write – for the last five years. At last the chance had come. She told Francis about 'Mrs Rochester' – and by June she had sold the option on her new novel to Deutsch. In a great rush of hope and confidence she wrote to Diana Athill, her editor: 'I hope to be able to submit the MSS of my new novel to André Deutsch by the end of this year – in six to nine months time – as a large part of it is already written.' She had promised to finish 'Mrs Rochester' at the latest by March 1958 – in fact, it was March 1966 before Deutsch finally received the completed typescript of *Wide Sargasso Sea*. Diana Athill, a writer herself, and soon to become a friend, never reproached her. But Jean, with her quixotic standards, her ignorance of the world, and her self-distrust, reproached herself endlessly. Several times she offered to give her advance back.

She was always the same – at one extreme or the other. If she was the least hesitant, she was utterly despondent; if she was at all hopeful, she was euphoric. When she was euphoric she felt the novel was almost done – half-written once before, and the rest safely in her head. But soon she saw it was not going to be like that at all. Mrs Rochester turned out to be the most difficult, ambitious, fascinating, elusive book she had ever written – 'a *demon* of a book'. 'Sometimes I am sure that it needs a demon to write it,' she wrote to Francis Wyndham. 'I live in hope – who knows? I may qualify.' It was about a mad mind, and she wanted to write it *madly*. That was dangerous – but she wrote the first version that way, with Antoinette as sole narrator. But then she thought, 'A mad girl speaking all the time is too much!': nobody would understand it. 'Besides, the old ideas, clarity, unity and so on – I can't get away from them – they are *valid*.' So she laboured to set Antoinette's disordered experience in a real, believable world, and to make smooth and plausible the relationship between them. That cost her enormous effort, because Antoinette's time was too far away from hers and she had no facts to steady her: 'One must have blind faith – like walking on water.' And how to do it? 'It can be done three ways,' she told Maryvonne. '(1) Straight, Childhood, Marriage, Finale told in 1st person' – that was her first version, and it wouldn't do.

Or it can be done (2) Man's point of view, (3) Woman's ditto both 1st person. Or it can be told in the third person with the writer as the Almighty. Well that is hard for me. I prefer direct thoughts and actions. I am doing (2). That is the end of that sermon –

This was the hardest thing of all for her – to put herself in the place of the Englishman, her old love, her old enemy. But she did. It exhausted her – 'that man is making me very *thin*' – but it produced her masterpiece.

For the first year she managed very little. She knew this could be her best book, and she was agitated by the fear that she must get it right, or it would be no good at all. She made 'about six toilsome efforts' to start, most of them with Antoinette's dream. She read and reread *Jane Eyre*, until it crept into her own writing and everything had to be scrapped. She tried to get herself back into the mood 'with the help of very bad drink. One day drunk, two days hung-over regular as clockwork.' But from mid-1958 she 'raced ahead without looking back'; and by January 1959 she had the first draft done – the story told by Antoinette. During 1959 she wrote it all over again, twice: first with Grace Poole as narrator (but 'I wasn't even sure how she'd talk or think'); finally with both Antoinette and Rochester as narrators, as it remains. From now on she could rewrite instead of write. It should have been easier – but over and over again she lapsed into uncertainty and struggle. 'Where to start? Who's to speak? What to cut?' she was still crying, in a letter to Francis Wyndham in 1960.

The difficulties of the book itself were fiendish enough. But of course there were others. In 1957 Maryvonne and her family had had to leave Indonesia and return to Holland, leaving behind them the effort and achievement of many years. Jean was always full of self-doubt and self-reproach as a mother; but now her frustration that she was too poor to help her daughter grew very painful, and became a permanent sorrow. Still, Maryvonne was young and practical and brave. A sadder and more hopeless worry was Max.

When Jean's renewal of hope and work had come in May 1957, Max still seemed all right. When she had had to be in bed that Christmas, he was 'very kind and dear' to her, and did all the chores. But later on she dated the decline in his health from that year. He began to suffer from giddiness, and from increasingly severe falls: in fact, he was having a series of mild strokes. From 1958, when he was seventy-five, he was ill every winter, rallying only briefly in the spring and summer. Most of the winter of 1959 he had to spend in bed, and Jean was ill too. They moved – to Perranporth, in north Cornwall – but Max did not really improve.

Jean was ageing and ill herself, often drunk, always struggling; but she took care of him. She who had needed Leslie's full-time care in order to write her earlier novels – she who had always felt a useless person, who had watched helplessly as her sister nursed their dying mother . . . But 'Once long ago,' she said, 'Max saved me from smashing' – and 'I've a good memory'. In the winter of 1961 Max had a spell in hospital. For the next two years Jean fought valiantly, even crazily, to keep him at home, because he hated hospital and was unhappy there. But the burden of taking care of him was immense, and in the end impossible. He was too heavy for her to lift; he became incontinent. By the autumn of 1963 she had to allow him to be taken back to hospital for good.

Her loyalty, affection and care for him in his last years must have made them less hard to bear for Max. But those years – really, his whole last decade and a half – are almost too sad to think of. First prison and disgrace; then terrible poverty he could do nothing to relieve; finally, prolonged illness and dependence. Max loved Jean and wanted to help her perhaps more than either of her other husbands, but he could help her least of all. He hadn't been able to give her even a year or two of comfort and pleasure, as Jean Lenglet had; he hadn't been able to help her in her work, as, for all their battles, Leslie had. (And Jean Lenglet too: he and Jean had exchanged ideas for stories, and they went on translating each other's work for many years.) 'He doesn't understand about books,' Jean told Maryvonne – especially about the agony of writing them. When he wasn't well (which was almost all the time now) she felt that he thought her struggles with *Wide Sargasso Sea* 'all a bore and a fuss about nothing'; she was certain that his real trouble was 'living in one room . . . (with me and book)'. In the tug of war between Max and *Wide Sargasso Sea*, Max often won. But even then

Jean's core of being a writer, which was a core of loneliness and separation, remained. That loneliness – and her drinking, her black moods, her anger – must have made his love for her painful too. 'Whatever you call me I love you and only you,' he wrote to her from hospital, in 1963. 'You deserve something better than me. I wish you had it.'

After the first draft of *Wide Sargasso Sea* was finished, in 1959, there were other distractions. Francis Wyndham helped her to sell several short stories; in the spring of 1960 she left the novel to finish the Holloway story she had been mulling over for so long. Then, also in 1960, she and Max made their final move. At last she would have what she had always longed for: a place of her own, a room to write in. Edward had bought a bungalow where the Hamers could live, in a small Devon village called Cheriton Fitzpaine.

'My gratitude is boundless,' Jean said; if she ever got to this 'new Jerusalem', she would never move again. She arrived there in September 1960. At first she was delighted with the tumble-down bungalow, peaceful and clean, surrounded by trees. But (as always) her happiness was short-lived. Max got worse, and Jean blamed it on the dampness of Cheriton Fitzpaine. It was cold and wet and dark, and there were icicles in the bathroom . . . '*Not my cup of tea*,' she said, almost straightaway. 'Needs some sugar!' But she never did move again.

She tried to get back to the novel, with the help now of pep pills as well as drink. She had terrible days, when she felt 'as if it had no meaning at all'; but by the summer of 1962 she was telling Francis Wyndham that Parts I and II were finished, and she would send them to him. He read them, and sent her letters full of praise, offers of help, suggestions. She was briefly buoyed up into certainty – 'I "see" this long delayed book at last and will have the courage to finish it, I trust' – but soon she had lost all confidence again: 'It is so bad in parts, isn't it? . . . I wish I had not sent you something unfinished.' This always happened: as soon as she had let something go, she became convinced it wasn't finished. 'I have such a *haunt* that they may publish the *skeleton* as my finished book,' she was still writing in 1964.

In August 1963, a Deutsch editor, Esther Whitby, came down to Cheriton Fitzpaine and typed out the whole of Jean's manuscript to date. That was just as well, for she had really only two more periods when she could work – a few months in the spring of 1964, and another few months from October 1965. From September 1963, when Max went into hospital for good, she was quite alone. And that she could never bear. When she was alone, she cracked: in London after her first affair; in Paris when Jean Lenglet was arrested; in Norfolk when Leslie was in the Air Force; in Beckenham when Max was chasing his mirage of riches. And now, as soon as Max was gone again, the signs of breakdown began to appear. 'I'm disapproved or worse of because *I try to write* (!!!)' she told Selma. People in the village said she was a witch; they were stealing from her . . . 'While Max was with me they didn't attack openly. *Now they are attacking.*' She felt she had only two friends left in the village: Sam Greenslade, a local farmer who was also the village taxi-driver; and the Rector, the Revd Francis Woodard. Years later she would say that Mr Woodard had seen her through her worst times in Devon, and that *Wide Sargasso Sea* was due to him.

In early 1964 came her working time, and Part I was published in *Art and Literature*. She told Francis Wyndham and Diana Athill once again that Parts I and II were finished, '*no more additions*' – though she quickly added, 'Delete perhaps . . .' But in the summer she was bad again. '*I will not crack*,' she said. But she did, so badly that she had to spend all of August in hospital. After that she accepted that *Wide Sargasso Sea* was nearly done. She went to London, to put the finishing touches to it there, and hand it over to Diana Athill herself – and in London she had a heart attack. For the next four months she was in hospitals and nursing homes, too weak to think of *Wide Sargasso Sea*. In March 1965 she was back in Cheriton Fitzpaine, having survived yet again. But Max was very ill. Her loneliness was like a nightmare – her courage had gone – she could not write. At last Maryvonne came to stay for a few weeks, and the worst was over. She took up the novel again; she sold three stories to *Art and Literature*. Then, at the beginning of March 1966, she had an urgent call from the hospital, and rushed to Max. Her brother-in-law, Alec Hamer, came to be with her; Maryvonne was on her way too. On 7 March she still wrote to Diana Athill that she had some additions to make to Part I, and deletions to Part II. But on that day Max died.

I feel that I've been walking a tightrope for a long, long time and have finally fallen off. I can't believe that I am so alone, and that there is no Max.

I've dreamt several times that I was going to have a baby – then I woke with relief.

Finally I dreamt that I was looking at the baby in a cradle – such a puny weak thing.

So the book must be finished, and that must be what I think about it really . . .

It's co *cold*.

ii. *Wide Sargasso Sea*

Wide Sargasso Sea is the story of how a white West Indian girl, cast out of her home and in love with a man who hates her, goes mad and dies in a cold, grey country she doesn't want to believe is England. It is Mrs Rochester's story; but it is also, of course, Jean's story. It is Jean's whole story, going right back to the beginning, and facing the worst truth about its end: that she was (sometimes) mad, and that the only escape from her madness is death.

Wide Sargasso Sea is in all senses Jean's culminating novel. In it her deepest themes come together perfectly: that the beauty of the world hides cruelty, that dream reveals reality, that there is no love. In it her dominating images come together too: colour and greyness, heat and cold, her lover and the man who hates her. Ever since *After Leaving Mr Mackenzie*, she had been especially haunted by the image of steps, or stairs, at the top of which her own future waits – an old forsaken woman, like the one on the floor above Julia: 'a shadow kept alive by a flame of hatred for someone who had long ago forgotten all about her'. In *Good Morning, Midnight* Sasha *is* at the top of the stairs. There is no higher floor than the fourth, which is hers; and the mad malevolent *commis voyageur* is not higher than her but her next-door neighbour on the same landing. Through the short stories the image of 'upstairs' recurs – associated with madness, in the high-barred windows of Laura's sanatorium in 'I Spy a Stranger'; associated with escape, in the similar windows of Selena's jail, in 'Let Them Call It Jazz'. Now, there is, of course, one floor higher than the highest floor: the attic. And that is where Antoinette is, in this last novel: where she is mad, and where she will escape. In all Jean's extraordinary work, this is surely the most extraordinary fact: that her own most personal image, the mad forsaken woman at the top of the stairs, lay in wait for her in Charlotte Brontë's book, written so long before. It is as though she and her heroines had been moving inexorably up the stairs towards Antoinette's attic all along. That fatedness, of course, she always felt. One great achievement of her last novel is that it makes us share that feeling.

Another is that she has succeeded in her efforts to make the book not just Antoinette's dream, but a drama; and 'to make the drama *possible*, convincing'. In her European novels there was something detached and dreamlike in the heroines' relation to the world: that was how Anna and Marya and Julia and Sasha saw things, and that was that. Although they completely convince us, therefore, that that is what life is like for them, mercifully few of us can feel that that is what life is like for us, for *anyone*. In *Wide Sargasso Sea* Jean persuasively sets her heroine's experience in a time and place where we believe life *could* have been like that for us, for anyone. Antoinette is paranoid – but we believe in her isolation, and in the malevolence and menace that she feels around her. She is mad, but we sympathize with her.

Jean achieved this by going out beyond Antoinette's

feelings, to realities of West Indian life in the early nine-
teenth century. That is why she found this novel so par-
ticularly hard: because, while still exploring the heroine's
dreamlike despair as brilliantly as ever, she also forced
herself outside Antoinette, to take in the largest cast of charac-
ters, the fullest descriptions of place, and the most crowded
canvas of events in all her novels. Above all, she forced
herself outside Antoinette's mind and feelings, into other
people's : especially, as we have already seen, into Rochester's. That is why Part II was 'so impossibly difficult' –
'Damned old Part II!!' For here she explores her recognition
that Rochester is not just a villain, and Antoinette not just a
victim. Rochester is, in *Wide Sargasso Sea*, very like Antoinette herself: a rejected child, alone in a strange land, afraid
of being hurt and exploited. It is his fear which makes him
unable to love and trust, except 'a little', as Christophine
says. But as much as he could, he loved Antoinette. '*Love
her as I did – oh yes I did*,' he admits to himself; and at the
end, when they have both suffered too much, he says to
her: 'I have made a terrible mistake. Forgive me.' He is no
mere triumphant destroyer of love, but himself destroyed
when he loses it: 'She had left me thirsty and all my life
would be thirst and longing for what I had lost before I
found it.' 'I knew him as a young man,' says his house-
keeper. 'He was gentle, generous, brave. His stay in the
West Indies has changed him out of all knowledge. He has
grey in his hair and misery in his eyes. Don't ask me to pity
anyone who had a hand in that.'

Jean fought through to an understanding of her old
enemy early in 1959, when she decided to tell Part II from

his point of view, and to 'stress the romantic side of his character – Poor man'. Then a suggestion from Diana Athill in 1963 made the whole book 'click into place' for her. She had given the lovers only a week of happiness before Daniel's letter arrives and turns everything to suspicion and hate. Diana Athill suggested it should be longer. Jean gave them four or five weeks instead: and 'As soon as I wrote that bit I realized that he must have fallen for her – and violently too.' The Rochester she had taken from *Jane Eyre* was '*all wrong*', 'a *heel*'.

> As soon as I saw that it all came to life. It had always been there . . . Mr Rochester is *not* a heel. He is a fierce and violent (Heathcliff) man who marries an alien creature, partly because his father arranges it, partly because he has had a bad attack of fever, partly no doubt for *lovely* mun, but most of all because he is *curious* about this girl – already half in love.
>
> Then . . . they get to this lovely lonely magic place and there is no 'half' at all.

For the first time, therefore, Jean faces the possibility that the 'bewildered English gent' loved and suffered too: that not only Anna and Julia loved and suffered, but Walter Jeffries, and Mr Mackenzie, and Neil James too. She no longer divides the world into strong and weak, with the strong exploiting the weak and getting off scot-free. She sees that everyone – even Daniel, the real villain of *Wide Sargasso Sea* – is in some way weak, and that it is through weakness rather than strength that cruelty and hurt enter the world. For the strong – Aunt Cora, and Christophine – are kind; and the things that have made Antoinette weak, rejection and isolation, fear and distrust, have oppressed Rochester and Daniel too. Rejection and fear make people, according to their natures, angry and violent (like Antoinette), envious and bitter (like Daniel), or cold and cruel (like Rochester). They make people unable to love and trust more than Christophine's 'little' – and this is as true of Antoinette as it is of Rochester. At the end of Part II Rochester feels that, if Antoinette had looked at him with love, 'I don't know what I would have said or done. In the balance – everything.' But – as Sasha did to René – she looks at him with hate instead. Then his own hate swings back and – like Sasha – she has lost her last chance, and is mad forever. With Sasha, Jean had faced her responsibility for losing someone like Jean Lenglet – a soldier of fortune, a gay but unreliable adventurer. With Antoinette she went back to her first and most painful loss, that of the rich, cautious, decent but self-preserving Englishman – someone like Lancelot. And at last she accepted her share of responsibility for that too.

Jean could recognize her fault, and blame her lover less, in Part II of *Wide Sargasso Sea*, because in Part I she had explored how the iron had entered her soul long ago, in childhood. For Antoinette suffers three terrible rejections long before she meets Rochester. She is rejected by her mother, who thinks only of her sick son, Pierre, and pushes Antoinette away 'as if she had decided for once and for all that I was useless to her'. She is rejected by the black people of her island: by the little girl who sings 'Go away white cockroach, go away, go away'; by the mob who sets fire to her home; worst of all, by Tia, who is briefly her only friend. And she is rejected by the new white people, who care only for money, and laugh at her.

They were very beautiful I thought and they wore such beautiful clothes that I looked away down at the flagstones and when they laughed – the gentleman laughed the loudest – I ran into the house, into my bedroom. There I stood with my back against the door and I could feel my heart all through me.

She does not like these white people, but they are the ones with ranks to close – 'They say when trouble comes close ranks, and so the white people did. But we were not in their ranks.' They own the houses with the thick walls and blazing fires; and they are the ones who, by refusing to let her in, consign her to the 'outside' forever.

Although Antoinette's story is so firmly set in the 1830s, her experiences of rejection and fear echo Jean's own feelings in childhood. We know that this is so from everything she wrote about her childhood: in *Voyage in the Dark*; in short stories, especially in her last collection; and above all in the last book she wrote, at the end of her life: *Smile Please*, her unfinished autobiography.

iii. *Smile Please*

From the start, she remembers, she felt different, the only fair one in a dark family; and from the start, that made her feel ugly. When she was twelve she met a young man called Mr Kennaway:

When he watches me I can see that he doesn't think I am pretty.

103

Oh God, let me be pretty when I grow up. Let me be, let me be. That's what is in his eyes: 'Not a pretty little girl.' He is English.

She imagined that she had seen the first Englishman's judgement of her, and she saw it in their eyes ever after. When she was an old lady (and still as beautiful as she had always really been), friends asked what she would like to be if she were reincarnated. She said without hesitation: 'I would like to be beautiful.'

Like Antoinette, she was a fearful child – afraid of the dark, of insects, of going to school. 'When I first knew I was to be sent to the convent as a day scholar I was very frightened. I cried, shrieked, clung to my mother and kicked up such a fuss that I didn't go.' Like Antoinette, too, she felt from the beginning that people didn't like her. Her Auntie B didn't like her; she thought her useless, because she couldn't (or wouldn't) sew. Auntie B was her mother's twin sister, and she felt the strong link between them. 'They would look at each other and both laugh quietly.' Her father would say, 'Oh I do like to see them laugh like that.' But she would feel: 'Could they possibly be laughing at me?'

Nonetheless, she admired Auntie B, who was serene and brave – so unlike herself. She admired them all, the ones who were unlike herself. Sometimes she took perverse pride in defying them; sometimes she was obstinate and angry. ('They are always expecting me to do things I don't want to do and I won't. I won't. I won't.') But that wasn't because she thought she was right and they were wrong – it was only because she couldn't change. Really she accepted their standards without question, and saw no route to happiness

apart from being accepted and adapted, pretty and successful. And so she only pretended to glory in her difference,
while secretly she prayed unceasingly for it to go away. She
refused to make friends with other outcasts, saying she preferred 'being an outcast by myself'. For they were right. Boys
should be strong, unlike Eddie Sawyer; girls *should* be neat
and pretty, unlike Gussie de Freitas. Eddie was her friend
anyway ('I loved, but sometimes despised him'); but she
would have nothing to do with Gussie. Making friends with
Gussie would have been making friends with herself, and
that she couldn't do.

For black people in general she felt her usual clash of
emotions. She envied their freedom; she admired their
health, their strength, their gaiety: 'They were more alive,
more a part of the place than we were.' But she was afraid
of them too – especially after the night of the Riot. Her
mother got her and her baby sister out of bed, and she
heard

a strange noise like animals howling but I knew it wasn't animals,
it was people and the noise came nearer and nearer.
My father said: 'They're perfectly harmless.'
'That's what you think,' my mother said.

The black people she knew well were different, 'in-
dividuals whom I liked or disliked'. The one she liked best
was a young girl called Francine, who became the model for
Francine in *Voyage in the Dark* and Tia in *Wide Sargasso Sea*.
But there was one she hated: Meta, 'my nurse and the
terror of my life'. Meta 'always seemed to be brooding over
some terrible, unforgettable wrong'. She taught the child

to fear zombis and soucriants, cockroaches and people – especially people. Jean never wrote about a person like Meta. Antoinette's nurse, Christophine, is her benign opposite, invented on the basis of happier memories. But Meta's malevolence crept into almost everyone she did write about, to create the general menace of her world. 'Meta showed me a world of fear and distrust,' she wrote, 'and I am still in that world.'

Long long ago – as long ago as for Antoinette – her mother's arms around her had been able to protect her and take away her fear. But not any more. Now she wasn't a baby any more, and she had to learn how to behave. Otherwise, 'I can't imagine what will become of you,' her mother said. She tried to shame her out of her fears: 'You're not my daughter if you're afraid of a horse. You're not my daughter if you're afraid of being seasick . . . In fact you're not my daughter.' She tried to punish her out of them. And she tried to frighten her out of them.

. . . I said to her the other day 'If you don't take care, you're going to be like your Aunt Clara. She was peculiar.' She said, 'What happened to her?' 'She was shut away,' I said. 'She had to be.' She said, 'If anyone ever shuts me away, even a little, I shall die.' I said, 'You say that. You're just talking.' 'Oh no,' she said, 'I am not just talking. I shall die.'

Her mother couldn't protect or change her, and when the new baby came she ceased to try. She loved babies. As long as her fourth child had been a baby she had loved even her. But now there was a fifth, and she drifted away. This fifth baby grew into a perfect little girl, neat and pretty, who did 'all she was expected to do and nothing that she wasn't'. This was Brenda, who became the model for Norah in *After Leaving Mr Mackenzie*. 'My mother didn't like me after Brenda was born,' Jean once said to Maryvonne. In *Smile Please* she wrote, 'I didn't hate her for supplanting me.' And, after she had understood Norah in *Mackenzie*, perhaps she didn't any more. But surely she did hate her sister when she was a child: and that would only have made her hate herself more.

It was her father she loved. For he did not try to change her; he loved even that thing in her which made her suddenly afraid and sad, for no reason. He even shared it:

... that time when I was crying about nothing and I thought he'd be wild, but he hugged me up and he didn't say anything. I had on a coral brooch and it got crushed. He hugged me up and then he said, 'I believe you're going to be like me, you poor little devil.' And that time when Mr Crowe said, 'You don't mean to say you're backing up that damned French monkey?' meaning the Governor, 'I've met some Englishmen,' he said, 'who were monkeys too.'

Her father loved words and books, as she did (her mother hated clever women); he liked odd, eccentric people, and defended them. He was Welsh, not English; he loved French, and wanted her to learn it. It was her mother – though she was Dominican – who was the English one, and tried to teach her children English ways. He was busy, and often distant, but when he noticed her he was kind and gentle. He stopped her lumpy English porridge for breakfast, and let her have an egg beaten up in hot milk and flavoured

107

with nutmeg instead. He let her give up her lessons in mathematics when he found her crying because she couldn't understand them. He told her that when he was fourteen he had run away from home, because people were unkind to him and he couldn't bear it. She loved him; and she was grateful to him for the rest of her life, because he taught her that 'if you can't bear something it's all right to run away'.

Here, in her father, were all the things Jean loved, but feared were not enough: words and books, kindness and fun, irresponsibility and weakness. In her mother were the things she needed, but the things she hated too: strength and protection; but also English superiority, philistinism and intolerance. She could only ever feel happy with people like her father, but only ever safe with people like her mother. The great battle in her between happiness and safety, which doomed her always to pick the wrong lovers and husbands, started here. Jean Lenglet, and Max too, were like her father: and so she liked and even loved them, but they could not protect her. In Lancelot, in Ford, and in Leslie she sought the safety her English mother had meant to her – but found too in all three (most in Ford, least in Leslie) her mother's coldness and disapproval. She always felt, like Antoinette, as though she were acting out a drama whose outcome had been decided long ago. And certainly her end was in her beginning, in her parents' strange, incompatible marriage.

The child of *Smile Please* has the same feelings, the same fears, even the same ideas as the old lady who wrote it. Gwen Williams became Jean Rhys, but she never really changed. As an artist she matured and grew, but as a person – in Diana Athill's words – 'she stuck emotionally' in childhood. Her heroines, and the half of herself they portrayed, were like children: self-absorbed, naïve, wilful but dependent; full of impossible dreams of love, beauty, riches; full of self-hatred for failing to live up to the grown-ups' ideals. Even the rest of her, the writer, was a child: a wise and brilliant child, who knew the most extraordinary things as if by magic, but ordinary things hardly at all. Like Antoinette – except that Antoinette dies when she is barely past twenty –she was stranded in a permanently prescient childhood. That was terrible, because this child was full of fears quite unreachable by reason; but it was also what she wanted: *never to grow up.* Grown-ups had jobs, dealt with business and money, owned houses, brought up children. She never did any of these things. And so her heroines wander through a very grown-up world, and see it extraordinarily clearly – and yet, somehow, not at all. They are, as she is, marooned in a child's imagination, where ordinary adult life is less than half understood. But a child's eyes also see straight through the surface of what grown-ups think is ordinary, to the life and death battles which lie beneath. Jean Rhys remained the lost and frightened child of *Smile Please* and of Part I of *Wide Sargasso Sea*: this brought her Antoinette's madness, but also the deep and narrow genius to tell her story.

CHAPTER SIX

Afterwards: 1966–79

i. *1966–79*

When *Wide Sargasso Sea* was finished, Jean was in her seventy-sixth year. Now at last she was 'rediscovered': and soon she was firmly established as the modern classic writer that, from a distance, the literary world in England, France, Holland, America, had long recognized her to be. *Wide Sargasso Sea* at last brought her recognition, prizes, money, friends. Her novels were all reissued, first by Deutsch, then by Penguin; she was made a Fellow of the Royal Society of Literature, she was even made a CBE. She was not rich, or even comfortable – to the end of her life, she never earned more than £5,000 a year. But she still lived in Edward's cottage; her daily needs were few: enough was left over for pleasure and treats, and she needn't have worried any more.

But of course she did worry. She had been poor, and terrified of poverty, for half a century, and it was too late to change now. In 1968, two years after the publication of *Wide Sargasso Sea*, her cottage was still bare, with wartime linoleum on the floor. She had no telephone or television, only a very old electric cooker, still no heating in the bathroom. With extraordinary fidelity to her nature, she left reality untouched and tried to escape only in imagination: a bare orange bulb on one wall, to give herself the illusion of sunshine ... Slowly the friends and the money that *Wide Sargasso Sea* had brought her transformed the cottage – with proper heating, a new cooker and fridge, a new bed, the sitting-room redecorated, all in white. She had been so impractical all her life that she had always been *uncomfortable*: her friends were touched by how happy and grateful a bit of warmth and comfort could make her.

But apart from brief happy moments, her success had come too late. There was no Max to share it with; and her long habit of anguish was far too deeply rooted. Why was it *now*, when she was old, that photographers lined up at her door? She would prepare herself with obsessive care, with a wig and make-up and beautiful clothes; she would be ill with apprehension, and secretly, crazily hopeful. But then she would see the photographs, and be in despair. In her mirror, with her sight blurred by gin – or beside a shaded lamp, looking into the eyes of a friend – she could still see her face as it had always been. But in a photograph she could not escape the truth. She was old, *old*, and she couldn't bear it.

All the journalists, students and professors made her miserable too. It was nearly fifty years since she had enjoyed watching Jean Lenglet's friends drift in and out of their room – and then she hadn't had to speak to them. Already when she was married to Leslie she had become a near-recluse; she had insisted on their telephone being ex-directory then, and she would only have one now on the same condition. She was terrified of people descending on her with only the brief warning a telephone allows; she needed time to prepare. Even then – however much time she had – she would meet her guests with a sense of being caught off guard, and tell them that they had come too early, or on the wrong day. She would always agree to see a new admirer – because she was bored, and hoped to find someone who could give her what she needed: type for her, or take her somewhere, or simply like her. But she was almost always disappointed, and always distressed at what they wrote. All too often she was entirely justified. But even when she wasn't, she would feel that they had made mistakes, and lied: and of course the truths would be forgotten, and only the lies remain.

Wide Sargasso Sea also lost her a friend: Selma Vaz Dias. Selma's love for Jean's work, her determined search for her and her enthusiastic, galvanizing support during the long years of neglect and poverty, had made Jean very fond of her, and hugely grateful. But Selma was a restless, unhappy, possessive person. Trouble was inevitable. It grew during the writing of *Wide Sargasso Sea*, when Selma began to press Jean for 'her' part of the novel, Antoinette's narrative, to adapt again for radio. Nothing made Jean more nervous than someone pressing her; she kept promising Selma the manuscript but never sent it. Then in 1963 Selma asked her to sign a paper about the broadcasting rights of *Voyage in the Dark*, *Good Morning, Midnight* and 'The First Mrs Rochester', and she did. A year and a half later, when she was in hospital after her heart attack, she signed again a more formal version of the agreement. She had signed away to Selma fifty per cent of the proceeds from all film, stage, television and radio adaptations of any of her books anywhere in the world, and sole artistic control. (In 1967, a mutual friend, the theatrical agent Margaret Ramsay, persuaded Selma to give up artistic control, and accept thirty-three and a third instead of fifty per cent; that is how things still stand today.)

Later, Jean said that when she signed the first time she was drunk, and thought the whole thing 'a joke'. But other things than drink were at work here too. Ever since that first letter from Lancelot's solicitor – 'Please acknowledge receipt and oblige' – legal and financial documents made her panic. She would sign to stop the panic; and to be polite and loyal to Selma. Then she would sign again, because she had promised. But now, when suddenly *Wide Sargasso Sea* was a success, and film directors enquired about the rights, she saw the consequences of her rash gesture. And just when she should have been enjoying the rewards of her long labour, she was anxious and miserable, trying to control the next juggernaut she had set in motion: a legal battle to challenge Selma's claim. Selma became one more person she shouldn't have trusted; one more person who had used her and let her down. And whatever else was true, she had. As Jean herself said, '. . . persecution maniacs (so called) always have been and usually still are, the victims of persecution'.

Inevitably, she would have to decline. But until about 1975, when she was eighty-five, she still fought through to many good moments. Writing still brought out her best self. It was as hard as it had always been, but it was her profession, her habit, her justification. She worked on a book of short stories, which was published in 1976; four years before she died, she set to work on the autobiography. When she worked on the stories she was already in her eighties, but she could still dictate (she now had to dictate) for up to six hours at a stretch in the afternoon. And even when she worked on the autobiography she was sometimes suddenly excited, absolutely sure and concentrated; she would suddenly dictate, apparently without thinking, simple, beautiful lines:

There were two breezes, the sea breeze and the land breeze. People said that they called the land breeze the undertaker breeze. But I never thought that. It smelt of flowers.

Until then, too, she could still enjoy her 'little happy minutes or sensations': a new dress or an old song, a beautiful day, a kind friend. Her friends – led by Francis Wyndham and Diana Athill, Sonia Orwell and Diana Melly – organized holidays for her in London every winter: she loved the shopping expeditions, the visits to the ballet and the theatre, the lovely meals in friends' houses and in restaurants. That was what she loved: seeing, hearing, touching beautiful things; feeling the excitement and uplift of an occasion – an outing – a fling. Then she was wonderful company, graceful and generous and full of fun; with exquisite manners, says Diana Athill, and a delightful sense of the absurd, say her Devon friends, Oliver and Mollie Stoner. Then she was the gay, laughing girl again, whom people had so rarely seen since Lancelot: the 'slant-eyed siren', Francis Wyndham says, 'with whom one could enjoy the full intensity of a treat as with no one else'. She would tell stories, and laugh until the tears came – about Mrs Hudnutt of the Château Juan les Pins, long ago, who thought that she was a re-incarnation of Madame Pompadour ... about an old lady who bowed whenever Satan's name was mentioned, and said when challenged, 'Well, you never know, one might as well be polite ...'

But in the end these moments became fewer and fewer. From 1975 on she could no longer be alone in a hotel, but wintered in flats, and finally in Diana Melly's home; from 1976 she had a nurse to care for her in Devon. Even her writing began to fail her. She didn't hear her voices any more, she lost faith in the value of her work. The hours of lucidity and courage to write that drink had given her shrank to half an hour, and then to nothing, and she was only drunk. When *Smile Please* was published soon after her death it was unfinished. It still contained Jean's inimitable voice, but with little breath left now: her strong emotion, strongly controlled had almost ebbed away.

Of her two weapons against despair, drink and writing, only drink was left. Writing had worked, because she had turned it against her real enemy, herself; but drink was a fifth column, and only released her demons of fear and distrust. They took hold of her and shook her mercilessly at the end. Drunk, she would laugh and cry, shout and curse; her obsessions would race through her mind as though they were afraid of being cheated by death. She would wipe her hand over her face as though to wipe away her anguish:

sometimes it would go, only to return a few minutes later. She retreated further and further into self-absorption, self-pity, and anger. She had always remembered feelings more than facts: now that she was old, and ill, and dying, she confused them utterly. People came to see her constantly, but as soon as they had gone she felt more alone than ever – and so she felt, and said, that no one ever came to see her. No matter how careful, loving and attentive people were, no matter how grateful she was – she would forget. The person in front of her would disappear and become *people*, all people – and people hated her, people stole her clothes, her manu-scripts, her money . . . 'She was enraged with *everyone*,' her nurse, Janet Bridger, says; but sometimes it was hard to remember it wasn't your fault. Sometimes Janet was reduced to tears, or David Plante to anger: then Jean's face would soften, and she would say, 'It's not you. It's the others.'

But it wasn't the others, it was herself. Isolation closed around her. She was old, she was dying, and she felt she had never lived. Over and over she checked her reflection in the mirror, but it was always the same. 'Found drowned,' she would say.

For many years, whenever her drinking or distress became too great, it would end in an accident or a fall. This happened more and more easily now. If a friend refused to give her any more to drink, she fell. When a tax inspector called, she said, 'I was so worried, I fell. I've been dying ever since.' During her last two or three years she fell more and more often. Finally, in March 1979 – two days before she was to take the typescript of *Smile Please* to Diana Athill in London – she fell again, and broke a hip. Despite her extreme frailty she had to have an operation. After it she had several mild strokes, and her consciousness faded slowly. It had taken Max's death for her to let go of *Wide Sargasso Sea*. Now, at last, she let herself go. She refused to speak or eat. She died on 14 May 1979, three months before her eighty-ninth birthday. *Smile Please* was published six months later.

ii. *Jean*

... very few people change after well say seven or seventeen. Not really.

They get *more* this or *more* that and of course look a bit different. But inside they are the same.

So wrote Jean at sixty-five, to Maryvonne. When she said 'people' she meant herself – and, as always on this subject, she was right. Now that she was very old she was *more* of this or that, but inside she was still the same. She still drank too much and ate too little; she still isolated herself and complained of isolation. Heaters, stoves, typewriters, tele-phones still baffled and threatened her; now even kettles and powder compacts joined in. She still lived the wrong sort of life in the wrong sort of place; she still did nothing about it but rage and moan – and then find the perfect words to mock herself, with sharp unsparing humour. She still hated rain and cold, discomfort and loneliness, nar-rowness and intolerance. She still loved clothes and make-up, excitement and romance. When a man who had been very gallant to her died, she said sadly, 'The last lover gone.' More than ever she loved mystery, 'trees, shadows, a shaded light'; more than ever she loved flowers, cats, romantic music – pretty, ephemeral things, whose easy early deaths moved her with a pity which was, again, for herself.

She was still torn between equal and opposite desires – for companionship and help but also for independence. 'I simply *cannot* understand,' she wrote, 'why so many people imagine that I'm a bit of rather battered ivy waving around – looking for any old oak to cling to, because I'm really a Savage Individualist.' She was both, as she had always been. She still felt that money came of itself, that love struck like lightning, that people simply gave her things: and equally that poverty, hate and loss just happened. And so she still felt that people, events, her own fate, swept her along against her will. She hated her passivity, but loved it, as she both hated and loved her paranoia: because they made her feel a victim, but let her feel innocent.

She was more and more withdrawn and reclusive. More and more her happiest moments were with new friends and new correspondents, to whom she could show her best and bravest side, and with whom she could feel new hope. But then one day they would see her drunk and angry, and she would see or imagine their disapproval: they knew her now, and her hope and control would be gone. The more they knew her, the worse it would be. And so she was worst with those she was closest to: those she loved, like Maryvonne; those she depended on, like the nurse and the friends who cared for her. She still felt she would be better dead, and she still clung to life.

It has always seemed a mystery to Jean's readers how she could have lived her whole adult life with her husbands, and yet write with such desperate authority about women who were utterly alone. The truth was that, even with her husbands – even with her daughter, even with her loving friends – she *was* alone. She was always alone. 'I always thought I was different,' she told David Plante. 'That I felt things they didn't feel.' Sometimes this difference shamed her, and filled her with fear; sometimes, when she saw meanness around her, it filled her with pride. She veered between exaltation and abasement; but whichever it was, it cut her off from other people. They were mysteries to her; she saw them as 'shadows', as 'trees walking'. She only knew herself. 'Other people are seen and heard and felt. Known? Not on your life.' She never knew what they did – even her husbands. She often wanted to give them things, but never knew what they wanted – even her daughter. And so when she wrote about people, she got them right, as Diana Athill says, 'by observing them accurately, never by motivation. She watched as a naturalist watches animals.' The only ones she could really understand and feel for were the ones who were most like her: women who were anxious or unhappy, and anxious or unhappy in the same ways as she was. This had happened with Germaine Richelot, when she was young; it happened with several friends of her old age. To the end she preferred the company of men, and went on hoping that the end of her isolation would come from them. But perhaps the closest she really came to escaping isolation was in her moments of sympathy with other women.

Sadly, however, she couldn't transform these moments of sympathy into any lasting feeling of company and solidarity.

In her fiction, she used the voices of dispossessed women – wanderers like the European heroines, Creoles like Antoinette, black women like Selena Davis; and many women, and many of the dispossessed, feel she spoke for them. And so she did – but quite unconsciously. As far as she knew, she spoke for herself: she had to struggle alone, because she felt alone. That is what makes her Jean Rhys. To think of her as a feminist, or a socialist, or any other 'ist' – except a solipsist or a subjectivist – is to miss her central and most tragic point. She was quite without the consolations – the shared burden, the hope of change – which any 'ism' brings. She was incapable of theory and action herself, and distrusted them in others; her view of the world was tragic and pessimistic. In her world the poor and weak are not better than the rich and strong: on the contrary, in their struggle to survive, they must be worse. Blacks are as materialistic and cruel as whites, women are more conventional and meaner than men, children can be meanest of all. And she did not believe that things would ever change, for the trouble lay deep in terrifying human nature, and *that* would never change. There would always be rich and poor, adapted and unadapted, happy and sad: she had flashes of pity and guilt, but mostly she just wanted to be one of the happy, rich and adapted ones herself. *Of course* feminists would like to hail her as a feminist, because her novels are a brilliant and graphic account of the traps that await dependent women, and what happens to them when they fall in. But Jean did not write about dependent women: she wrote about herself. She had seen the warders, the governor, the doctor, in Holloway – all women, and each one worse than the next.

'I did think of the suffragettes,' she wrote. 'Result of all their sacrifices? The woman doctor!!! Really human effort is futile.' After that, it is no wonder that whenever she read a review that was even mildly feminist, she laughed and tore it up. Her solipsism and her pessimism combined to make her writing exactly what she said it was: a quest for self-knowledge, and nothing to do with anyone else.

She wrote to understand her isolation – and then she had to go on being isolated in order to write. She blamed writing for keeping her alone, and for making her use other people; often she felt it hadn't been worth it. Putting her writing first had cost her everything, even her child. 'Jean gave me up because her writing was more important,' Maryvonne says. *But the isolation came first* – it was what drove her to write, and to sacrifice everything to the possibility of going on writing.

This takes us to the heart of Jean's feeling about her writing, which like all her feelings was a contradiction, a mixture of love and hate. It was, she recognized, 'my truth and why I was born'; only through writing could she 'earn death'. And yet she dreaded it intensely, and wished only that she wouldn't have to do it. In order to do it she had to abandon herself to her unconscious mind – to dreams and voices and drink; to the feeling that she was a pen in someone else's hand. Then when it was done she couldn't let it go, or let anyone see it, without agonies of doubt and indecision . . . All this happened because it was here that she faced the truth about herself and her isolation: that it wouldn't end because *she* wouldn't let it end; that people wouldn't love and trust her, because *she* wouldn't love and trust them. But this knowledge was unbearable. However painful they were, she preferred the illusions of her paranoia, in which she was an innocent and beautiful victim of other people's cruelty. And so she was unhappy with writing, and unhappy with people who liked her books; alas, she would be unhappiest of all with us, who understand what she confessed about herself in them. She could only imagine being loved for those terrible illusions, her absolute innocence and beauty. She couldn't imagine that she could be loved instead for her courage, her honesty, her supreme artistry. But she is.

Her only happy times came when she could, briefly, believe that she was loved: by both her parents, on her sixth birthday; by her father, as she mixed his cocktails in the evening; by the Richelots; by Lancelot. But 'after well say seven or seventeen', it was all over: love had turned into rejection and loss, and she was trapped in the prison of her isolated, unloved self, as Antoinette is trapped in her attic. Only once, in France, had she glimpsed an escape from this prison. She described it several times, in fragments she always headed 'The Forlorn Hope', but never published.

It was on a hot summer afternoon; she was walking along the road from Théoule to Cannes. When she came to a place called La Napoule, she turned off the road and went to sit by the sea for a while. That was when it happened – 'a *certainty* of joy, and terrific, terrific happiness, not only for me, but for everyone'. She thought, 'Why do I hate people? They're not hateful.' It had happened because

I no longer existed. I was the wind and the blue sea. The 'I' was left behind – a horrible dream of prison . . .

The escape was what she had always thought it was, in everything she wrote, from her first diary to *Wide Sargasso Sea*: death. Now that she was very old, she had two visions of her life after death. One was in the story called 'I Used to Live Here Once': she returns to Dominica as a ghost, and two children run away from her, afraid. In the other she felt differently: 'There must be something after. You see, we have such longings, such great longings, they can't be for nothing . . .' After all the suffering her art so bravely showed us, we must hope that she felt at the end not the final homelessness of her story, but the escape into joy of La Napoule.

Published Works of Jean Rhys

The Left Bank and Other Stories, with a preface by Ford Madox Ford, Jonathan Cape, London, 1927; Harper & Brothers, New York, 1927.

Postures (later known as *Quartet*), Chatto & Windus, London, 1928; Simon & Schuster, New York, 1929. Reissued (as *Quartet*) by André Deutsch, London, 1969, and Harper & Row, New York, 1971. *Quartet* published by Penguin, 1973.

After Leaving Mr Mackenzie, Jonathan Cape, London 1930; Alfred A. Knopf, New York, 1931. Reissued by André Deutsch, London, 1969, and Harper & Row, New York, 1972. Published by Penguin, 1971.

Voyage in the Dark, Constable, London, 1934; William Morrow, New York, 1935. Reissued by André Deutsch, London, 1967, and W. W. Norton, New York, 1968. Published by Penguin, 1969.

Good Morning, Midnight, Constable, London, 1939; Harper & Row, New York, 1970. Reissued by André Deutsch, London, 1967. Published by Penguin, 1968.

BIBLIOGRAPHY

Wide Sargasso Sea, André Deutsch, London 1966; W. W. Norton, New York, 1967. Published by Penguin 1968.

Tigers are Better Looking, André Deutsch, London, 1968; Harper & Row, New York, 1974. Published by Penguin, 1973.

'I Spy a Stranger' and 'Temps Perdi', Penguin Modern Stories 1, London, 1969.

Sleep It Off Lady, André Deutsch, London, 1976; Harper & Row, New York, 1976. Published by Penguin, 1979.

Smile Please, André Deutsch, London, 1979; Harper & Row, New York, 1979. Published by Penguin, 1981.

Further Reading

Louis James, *Jean Rhys*, Critical Studies of Caribbean Writers, Longman, London, 1978.

Helen Nebeker, *Jean Rhys: Woman in Passage*, Women's Publications, Montreal, 1981.

Edward de Neve, *Barred*, Desmond Harmsworth, London, 1932.

David Plante, *Difficult Women*, Victor Gollancz, London, 1983.

Thomas F. Staley, *Jean Rhys: A Critical Study*, Macmillan, London, 1979.

Elizabeth Vreeland, 'Jean Rhys', *Paris Review*, New York, Fall 1979.

Francis Wyndham and Diana Melly (eds.), *Jean Rhys: Letters 1931–1966*, André Deutsch, London, 1984.